INYAFACE

@

TWAT.COMM

tom law's posts on twitter for 2017

ISBN   9780648226802

Copyright © 2018 Tom Law

Disclaimer: All materials in this publication are entirely the thoughts and the opinions of the writer Tom Law and do not reflect those of the publishers, producers or distributors.

Published in Australia by:
Longership Publishing Australia
Swifts Creek Victoria 3896 AUSTRALIA
ABN 73446736413
email: longership@email.com
First published in Australia 2018
Copyright © Tom Law   2018
Cover design: Tom Law

The right of Tom Law to be identified as the Author of the Work has been asserted in accordance with the Copyright, Designs and Patents Act 1988.

All rights reserved. No part of this publication may be reproduced, stored in a retrieval system, or transmitted in any form or by means without the prior written permission of the publisher, nor be otherwise circulated in any form of binding or cover other than that in which it is published and without a similar condition being imposed on the subsequent purchaser.

Law, Tom
INYAFACE@TWAT.COMM
ISBN: 9780648226802
pp 276

INYAFACE
@
TWAT.COMM

tom law's posts on twitter for 2017

Longership Publishing Australia

Contents

Forward		*11*
I	*Australia*	*12*
II	*America*	*101*
III	*Britain*	*133*
IV	*Wars*	*159*
V	*Guns*	*197*
VI	*Climate & Environment*	*223*
VII	*General*	*235*
VIII	*Cruel, Nasty and Definitely NOT Mine!*	*259*
Refer		*268*
Other Titles by Tom Law		*269*

Forward

This is by no means an intellectual work nor is it to be taken too seriously! The majority of the following tweets were placed on the longership twitter account over the period November 2016 to November 2017 and reflect some of the political nonsense that went on in social media over that time period. A colleague suggested that some were a little too much "in ya face!" Whereas some superstars have followers in the millions, Tom Law did not ever reach even 500 followers ha ha! The problem is that any individual's bag of political views, morality and values covers a spectrum with only a portion of overlap with that of others! So where there is agreement one day, there is disharmony on another with the result of followers coming and going. But to Tom that is not of great importance for he enjoyed creating his tweets for both pleasure and on many occasions to just 'let off steam'! It has been suggested that during the US Presidential election period at the end of 2016, the Russians paid for and spent time creating millions of tweets and facebook posts with false and objectionable materials to favour one candidate over another. Whether this was true and whether it had any serious effect on the election outcome is debateable. Personally I think it is an absurd claim. But people must judge for themselves and social media is just a part of the information sledge hammer that we all suffer (that is if we choose!)

I have included just a handful of examples of tweets in Chapter VIII that are NOT my own creations and of which I found to be extremely offensive. You might ask "why they are included?" Well basically to provide the reader with the worst aspects of an UNCHECKED social media platform and to question its total freedom and disregard to common decency. One hopes some tighter rules will be applied in the future!

Tom Law, December 2017

I   *Australia*

It has been a tumultuous year in Australian politics with such debacles as the dual citizenship fiasco causing heads to roll and the pathetic antics of Pauline Handsome and her One White Nation party. I think the worst of her actions was the wearing of the full female Muslim garb into the Senate and her call to ban the burger! What McDonalds thought of all this is anyone's guess? The viewing of Parliament on the telly is a constant embarrassment for any true blue Ozzie to watch with the constant bickering and slagging off across the chamber floor!

The Manus Island Detention Centre has also been a bewildering exercise possibly breaking a whole gamut of international law. It is hard to fathom why the Australian Government has kept people in these gulags (Manus and Nauru) for in excess of four years? It is certainly not the action of a modern democracy and supposedly civilised nation! My close friend who is a member of the Renewable Energy Party was a bit taken aback by some of my tweets referring them to be over the top and more than a little 'in ya face'! Hence the title of the collection for posterity! Labor has constantly called on the Government for a Royal Commission into the Banks as well as demanding Google and the big mining companies to commence paying 'real tax' on their Australian earnings. Our Armed Forces have continued to meddle in overseas conflicts as well as dropping bombs on Arab cities contributing to thousands of civilian casualties and millions of refugees.. and yet we are constantly outraged by the occasional mosquito bite of retaliation by Muslim extremists in the West. We live in a crazy world in crazy times! Lastly we have suffered the electricity problems of high cost and irregular supply. BUT everyone seems to forget WHO sold off most of the utilities in the first place! Privatise, Privatise, Privatise, Privatise.. seems to be the constant catchphrase of the day!

put her behind bars !!

I still agree with David Stratton and his views on "Romper Stomper", a film written and directed by Geoffrey Wright

... a trashy film that still continues to do DAMAGE in the Australian community !!

Tom Law

ADF to purchase 20 drones at nearly $500,000 each !

< this one only $235

Meanwhile many Australians still living on streets in cardboard boxes ... including some ex-servicemen !
GETTING OUR PRIORITIES !!

FREEDOM OF VOMIT SPEECH

... and will this man allow US Nazi Mike Enoch to enter Australia ?

... after all, he let the Dutch Nazi Wilders in a year ago !

OUR POLIES LEAN OVER BACKWARDS FOR TRADE AND FAVOURS TO CHINA

... NOW THEY ARE COMPLAINING THAT THE COMMOS ARE INTO EVERYTHING !

WHAT DID THEY EXPECT ?

UNTIL CHINA LEARNS GREATER RESPECT AND BEHAVES FAVOURABLY WE NEED TO DISENGAGE & EXTRICATE

GET THEM OUT !

* end ALL trade
* send home students
* nationalise Chinese companies
* end ALL immigration of Chinese nationals
* halt to Chinese ownership of property here

TAX DOMINOE GAME !

"NO... DON'T HIT HIM SCOTT !"

OZZIE BATTLER

"YES, A MUCH BETTER WAY SCOTTY MY BOY.... WELL DONE !!"

BANKS   OZZIE BATTLER

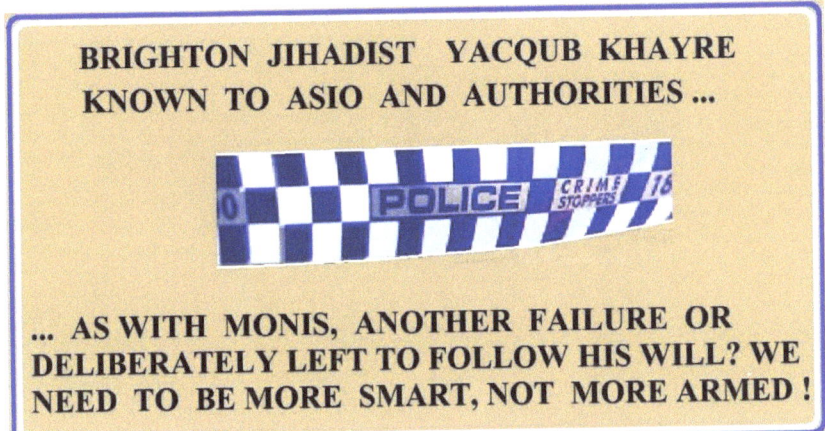

BRIGHTON JIHADIST YACQUB KHAYRE KNOWN TO ASIO AND AUTHORITIES ...

... AS WITH MONIS, ANOTHER FAILURE OR DELIBERATELY LEFT TO FOLLOW HIS WILL? WE NEED TO BE MORE SMART, NOT MORE ARMED !

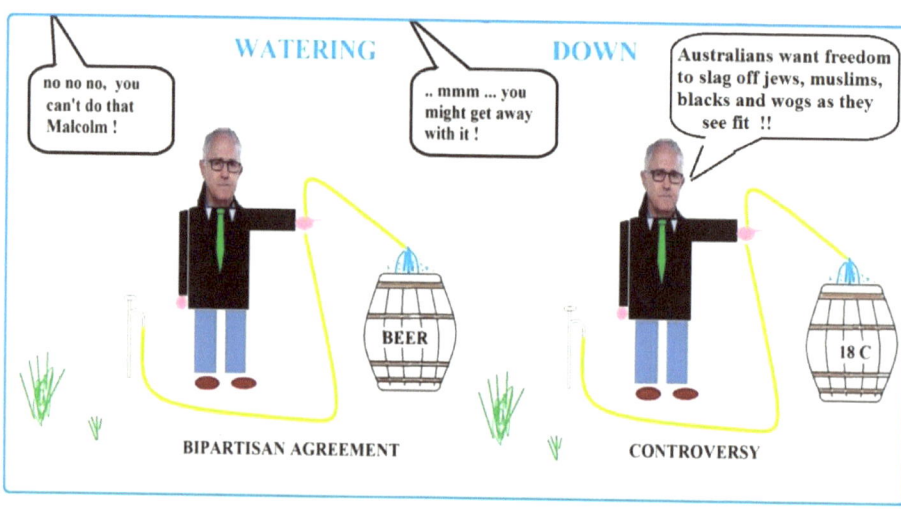

EASY TO BLAME TEACHERS FOR PERCEIVED LACK OF STUDENT IMPROVEMENT

PERHAPS SENATOR LAMBY SHOULD LOOK TO CURRENT VALUES OF SOCIETY ALSO... FAMILY BREAKDOWNS, DRUGS, LACK OF RESPECT, TV etc. etc.

---

britishmanhood asks:

WHY WOULD AN AUSTRALIAN NAZI GROUP CALL THEMSELVES

 'DINGOES' ?

THE DINGO IS A NATIVE OF AUSTRALIA AND HAS NO RELATION TO WHITE PEOPLE !

WHY NOT CHANGE IT TO
'MORONIC DRONGOES'
OR
'MORONGOES'

KEEPING AUSTRALIA SAFE

SINCE 1979 THE RUSSIANS AND THE WEST HAVE SUCCESSFULLY CREATED 40 MILLION REFUGEES AND KILLED BETWEEN FOUR AND FIVE MILLION PEOPLE, MANY INNOCENT WOMEN AND CHILDREN. THIS PROXY WAR BETWEEN RUSSIA AND THE WEST GOES ON WITH THE LIKELYHOOD OF MANY MORE DEATHS AND REFUGEES AND DESTRUCTION OF CITIES AND INFRASTRUCTURE OF NATIONS. THE ARMAMENTS AND WEAPONS MANUFACTURERS AND THEIR EVIL SALES PERSONS HAVE ALL THIS BLOOD ON THEIR HANDS. WE HAVE SUCCESSFULLY FANNED THE FLAME OF HATRED AMONG NATIONS AND RELIGIOUS GROUPS THAT CANNOT NOW BE EXTINGUISHED! FOR OUR PART IT IS NOT POSSIBLE TO KEEP OUR NATION SAFE FOR A LONG TIME INTO THE FUTURE.

THE ONLY THING LEFT FOR GOVERNMENTS TO DO IS TO SLOWLY BUT SURELY ERODE OUR FREEDOMS UNDER THE BANNER "KEEPING US ALL SAFE !"

TOM LAW 2017

DOES 'SHOOT TO KILL' LESSEN OUR DEMOCRACY ?

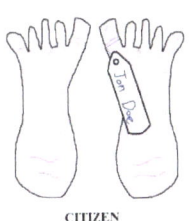
CITIZEN

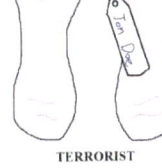
TERRORIST

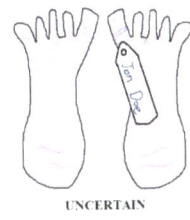
UNCERTAIN

AND WHEN IS IT CONSIDERED MURDER ?

... and will this man be called before Magistrate Charles Rozencwajg for his racial comments against Lebanese muslims ?

Terror hearing in Melbourne pathetic !!

AGAINST MY BETTER JUDGEMENT, I WOULD SUPPORT THE ADANI COAL MINE TO GO AHEAD IF THE FEDERAL GOVT. INITIATED A PURELY AUSTRALIAN CAR INDUSTRY... PREFERABLY ELECTRIC... WE CAN DO IT !!

... OTHERWISE FORGET IT !!

THIS BOOK IS ACTUALLY A LOAD OF CRAP ...

NOTHING
TO DO WITH ISLAM?

Investigating the West's Most Dangerous Blind Spot

PETER TOWNSEND

THE RESURGENCE OF THE EXTREME RIGHT IS OUR TRUE BLINDSPOT !

May 2017

REVOLUTIONARY BUDGET: ... "AUSSIES LOOK AFTER THEIR MATES" says Mr Morrison

Australians owning more than <u>three</u> houses are to <u>give away</u> their excess houses to the needy and homeless !!

Australians owning more than <u>three</u> appartments are also to <u>give away</u> their excess appartments to the needy and homeless !!

Thankyou Mr Morrison for such a generous and empathetic deal !

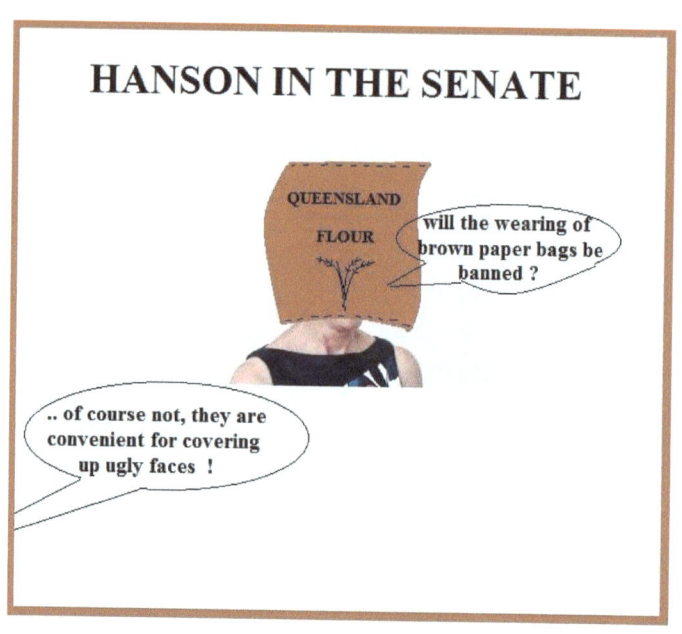

OUR HEAD OF STATE IS BRITISH

OUR FLAG IS PART BRITISH

DUAL CITIZENSHIP WITH BRITAIN AND NEW ZEALAND SHOULD BE EXEMPT... AFTER ALL, ARE <u>THEY</u> REALLY FOREIGN ?

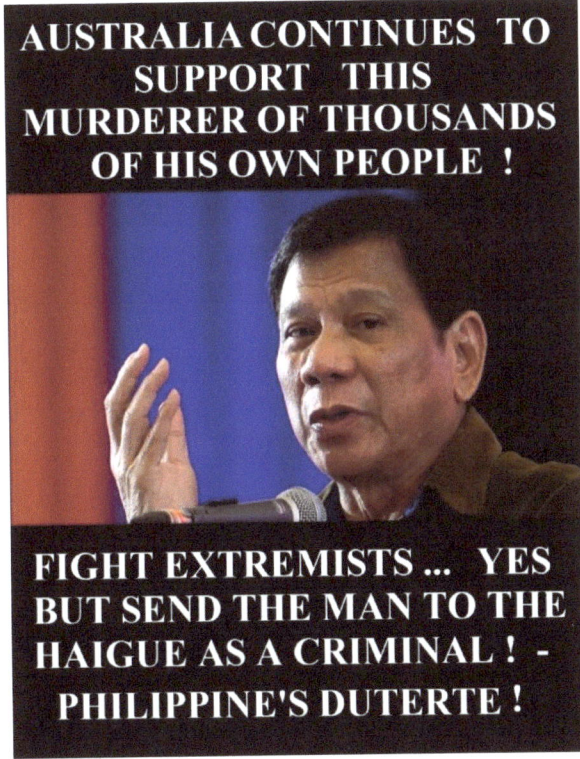

... almost devil like !

... heaven save us !!

PLEASE DEAR GOVERNMENT:

LIMIT MAXIMUM INCOME

(INCLUDING BONUSES) OF

CEOs AND OTHER EXECUTIVES

TO 20x THE AVERAGE WAGE.

ABOVE THIS TAX RATE TO BE

        100%

CURRENTLY:

WESTFIELD CORP   >$26 million

MAQUARIE GROUP   >$25 million

DOMINOS PIZZA   >$21 million

DISGRACEFULL GREED !!

HANSON HAS A VALID POINT !

PAULINE HANSON HAS BROUGHT UP AN INTERESTING POINT ABOUT STUDENTS WITH LEARNING PROBLEMS IN THE CLASSROOM... THIS IS A COMPLEX ISSUE WITH NO BLACK AND WHITE ANSWER AND CERTAINLY NO EMOTIONAL RESPONSE! AS A SECONDARY TEACHER OF MORE THAN FORTY YEARS STANDING I GIVE THIS ADVICE:

"EACH CASE HAS TO BE JUDGED SEPARATELY ON ITS OWN MERIT. WHERE A CHILD IS TOO DISRUPTIVE TO THE CLASS AS A WHOLE CONSTANTLY, THEN THE CHILD MUST BE REMOVED. HAVING SAID THAT, IT SHOULD ALWAYS BE A LAST RESORT AFTER ALL OTHER AVENUES HAVE BEEN TRIED! THE CLASSROOM TEACHER MUST BE SUPPORTED ON THIS ISSUE AS IT IS HER/HIS FINAL RESPONSIBLITY FOR LEARNING TO TAKE PLACE."

Tom Law.

Notes: (i) Ms Hanson's stance is more extreme than this.
(ii) I normally NEVER agree with her rubbish!

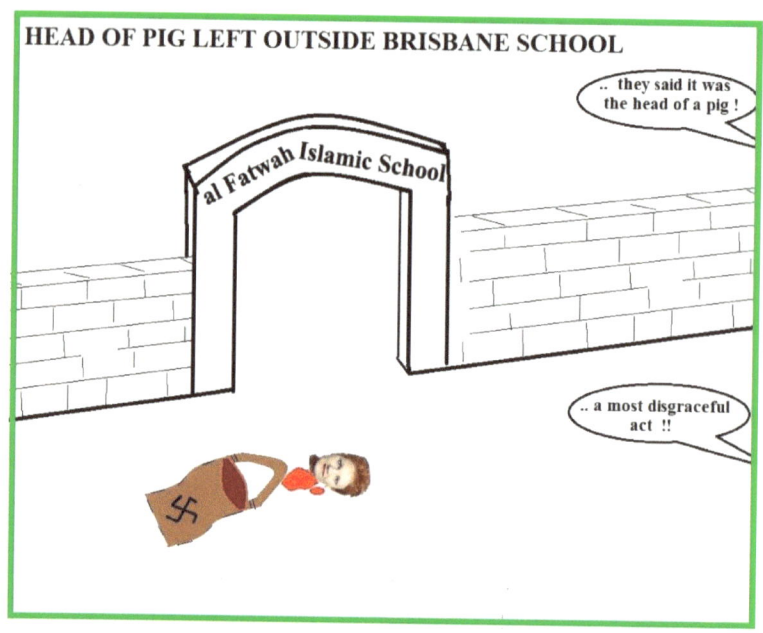

SUPER HORSESHIT FROM VIC POLICE !

WE ARE SO FAR UP AMERICA'S BUM THAT WE CANNOT SEE IN THE DARK !

VIC GOVERNMENT USING "SCARE TACTICS" AND HEAVY METHODS TO

INTIMIDATE THE POPULATION WITH US WEAPONS TRAINING... WHAT IS

THEIR TRUE AGENDA ?

WHERE ARE THE TERRORISTS ?

WHERE ARE ALL THE SCHOOL SHOOTING ATTACKS ?

THE LINDT CAFE SIEGE WAS A SET-UP BY ASIO AND THE NSW POLICE !

IT IS ASSISTANT COMMISSIONER CASEY THAT IS LIVING IN A

DIFFERENT WORLD, ... A WORLD WE DON'T WISH TO SHARE WITH HIM !

STAR WARS STORM TROOPERS ARE NOT GOING TO KEEP THE COMMUNITY SAFE ! NEITHER WILL US MODELS OF POLICING KEEP THE COMMUNITY SAFE ! TOM LAW.

gunsoffcops.com

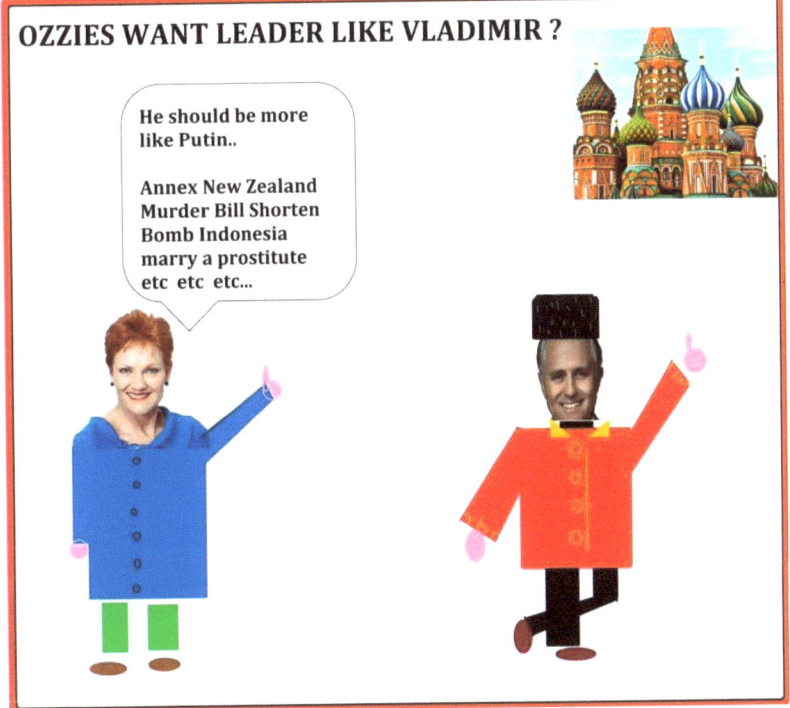

Wearing of Brown Paper Bag in the Senate stays !

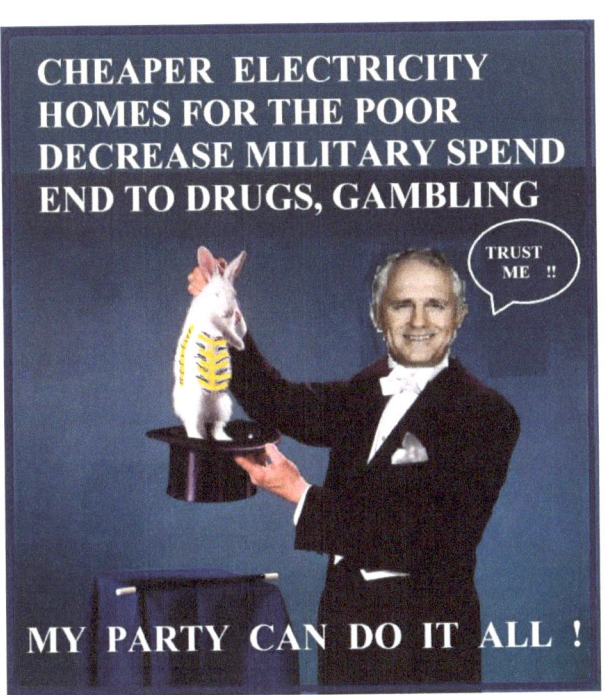

DUAL CITIZENSHIP OF AUSTRALIAN CITIZENS

IF A CITIZEN OF AUSTRALIA WAS BORN IN AUSTRALIA OR WAS ORDAINED AS A CITIZEN OF AUSTRALIA DUE TO HIS OR HER PARENTAGE THEN THAT CITIZEN CAN ONLY BE CONSIDERED TO POSSESS DUAL CITIZENSHIP ON CONDITION

THAT THE FOREIGN CITIZENSHIP HAS BEEN FORMALY APPLIED FOR AND GRANTED. A FOREIGN GOVERNMENT CANNOT INSIST THAT AN AUSTRALIAN BORN CITIZEN IS A CITIZEN OF ITS COUNTRY UNLESS SUCH

AN APPLICATION HAS BEEN FORMALY SUBMITTED AND CONSIDERED BY THE FOREIGN COUNTRY. HAVING THE POTENTIAL OF CITIZENSHIP OF ANOTHER COUNTRY IS IRRELEVANT .

Retweet

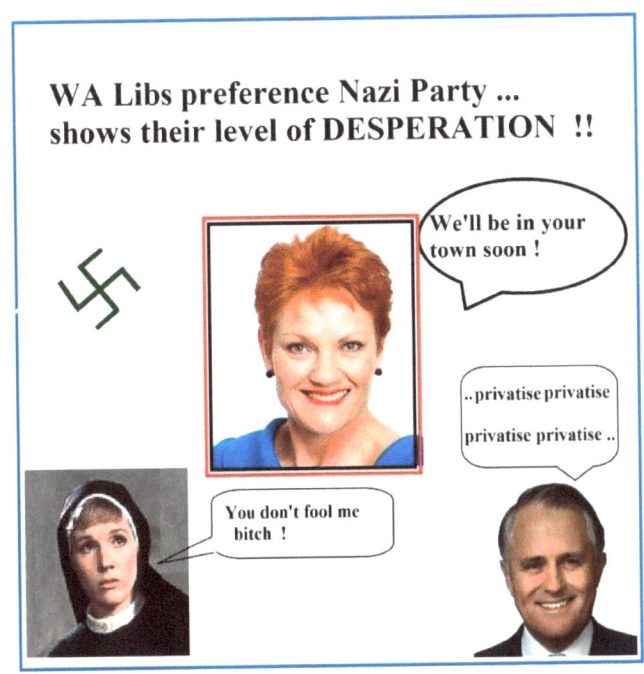

SACRIFICING OF A SACRED COW?

BENDIGO · ANZ · COMMB · NAB · Westpac

"can pay for mein neu office!"

".. we've milked the cows, now maybe we need to kill one!"

".. and help pay for expensive subs and overseas wars?"

'You will never defeat us'

ACTU boss Sally McManus issues a call to arms for true believers in a spray against "union-bashing governments" and media.

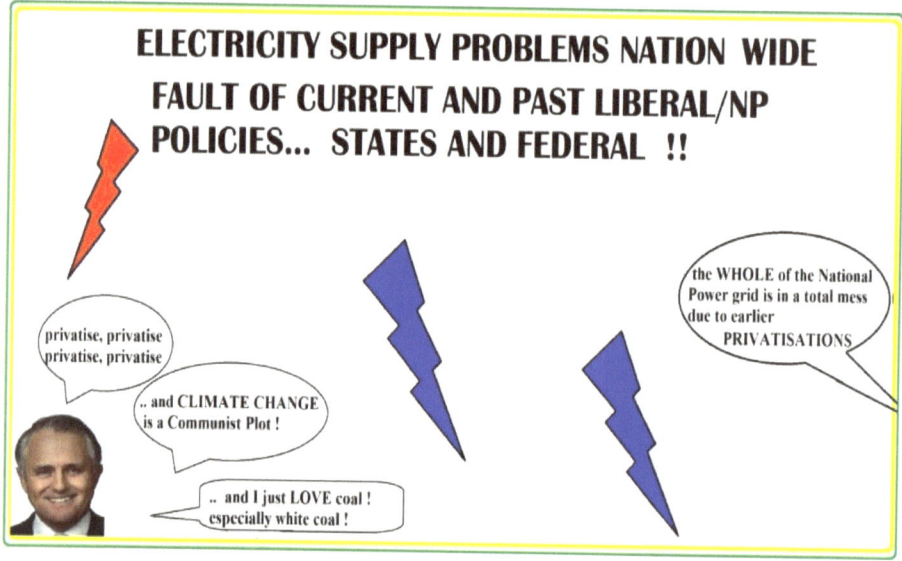

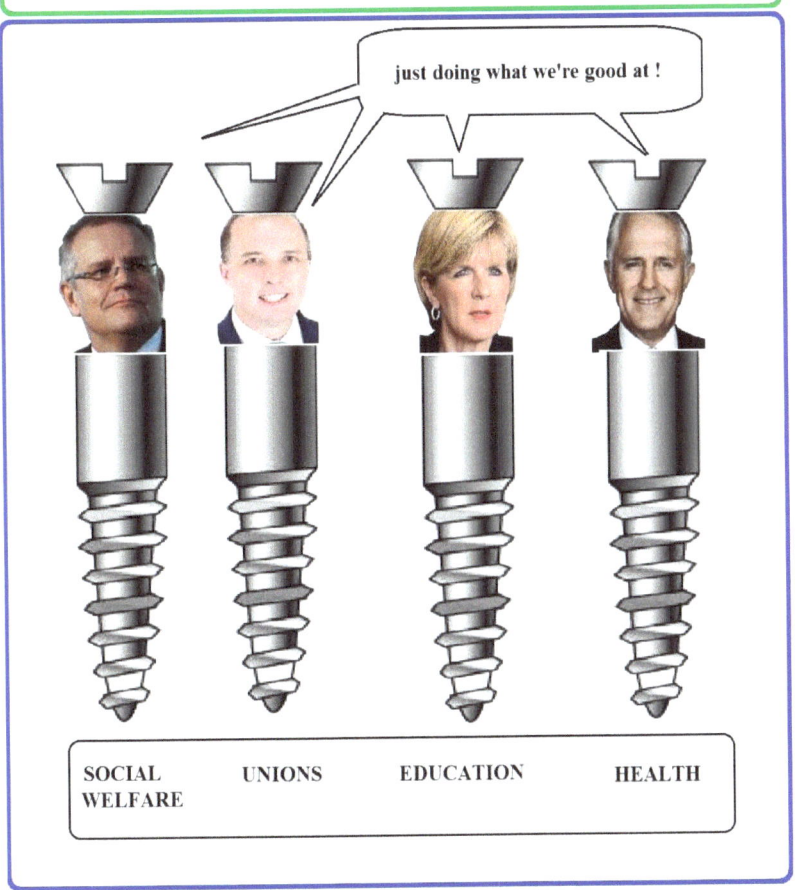

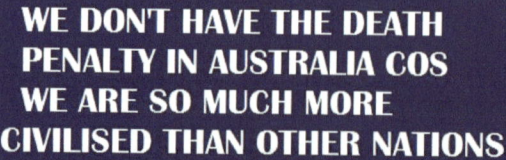

WHEN WILL NSW COPS STOP SHOOTING DEAD MEMBERS OF THE PUBLIC?

TAKE AWAY THEIR GUNS AND TASERS NOW!

longership.com
gunsoffcops   by tom law

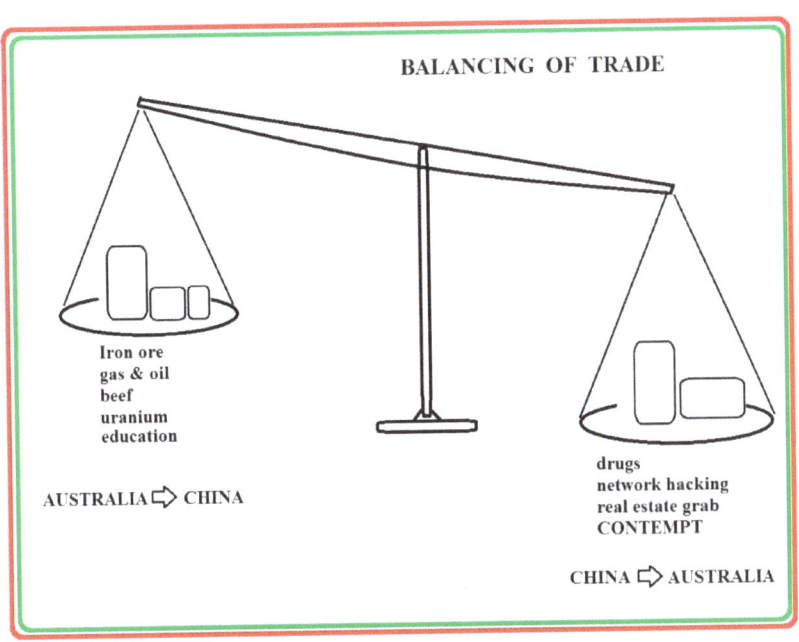

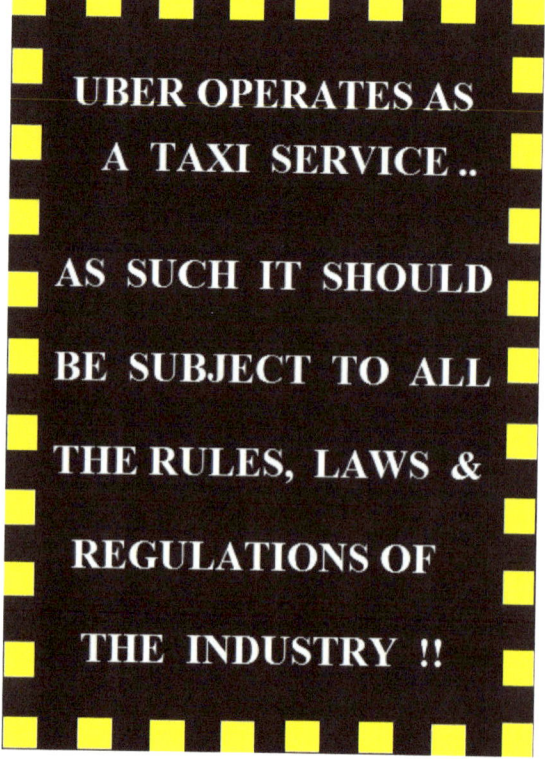

**YARRA CITY COUNCIL
DARREBIN CITY COUNCIL**

**SACK THEM ALL NOW !
OR SEND THEM BACK TO
MARS & VENUS FROM WHERE
THEY ORIGINATED !!**

... listen all you poor Ozzies, me mates own plenty of houses and appartments so why don't you just pay rent and shut uppa your face !!

Scott Morrison
.. solution to homelessness ??

Hopefully NOT **Coming Soon**

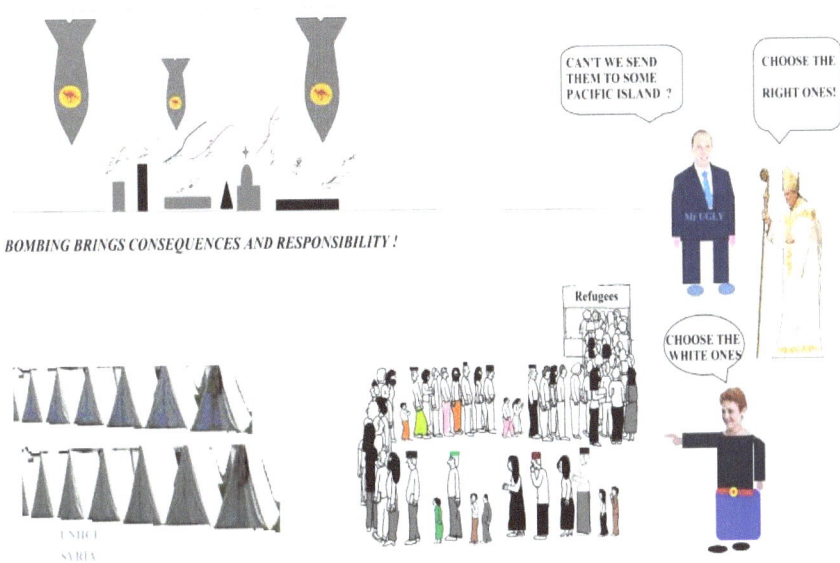

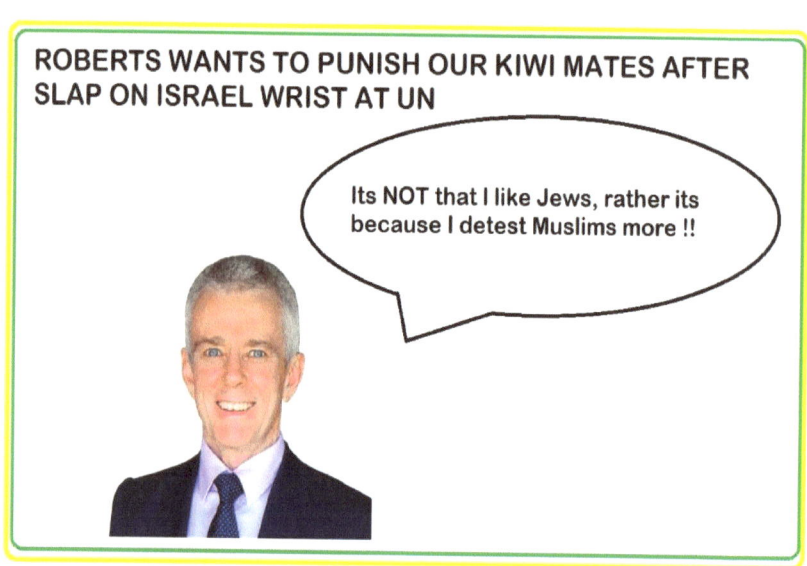

"THE'RE MAKING MUGS OUT OF ALL OF US!"

The One Nation leader says the questions on the current test are childish, laughable and many Australians wouldn't even know the answers!

... obviously the plot is to bring in migrants that are TOO SMART !!

... NO WORRIES MATE!

THANKS FOR THE PORT OF DARWIN, ALL THAT URANIUM, GAS, COAL, IRON ORE ....

NO SLUSH HERE!

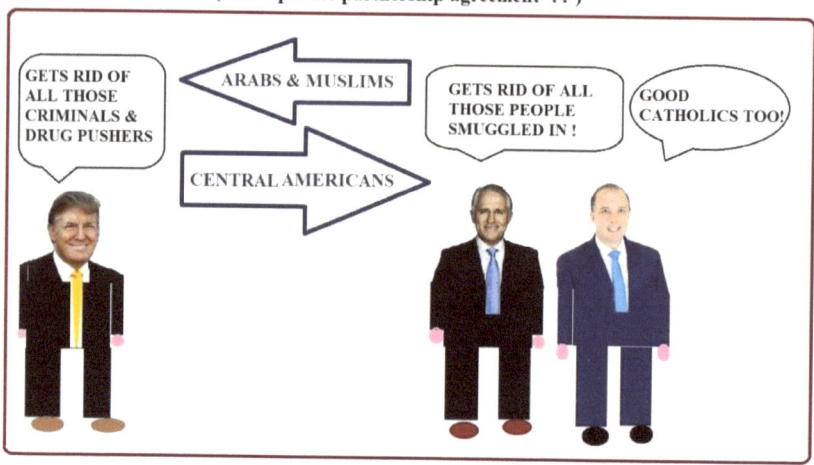

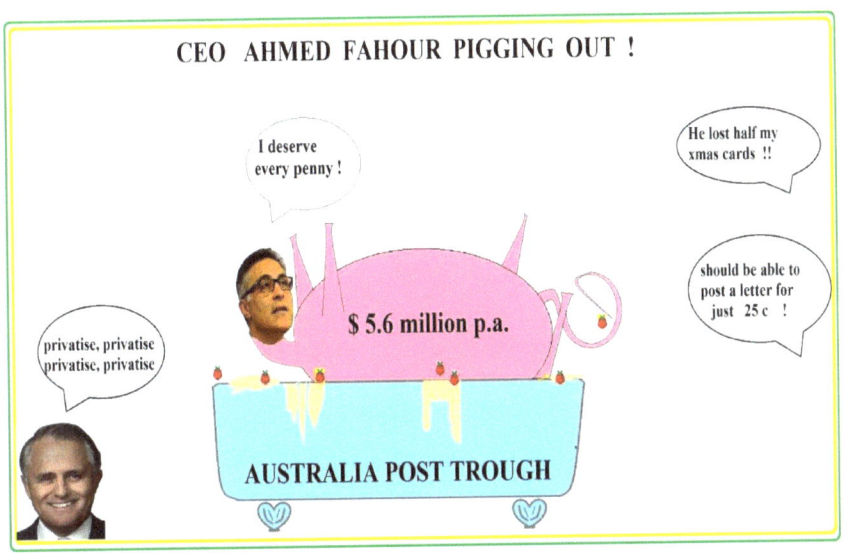

… so many pigging out in the cream !

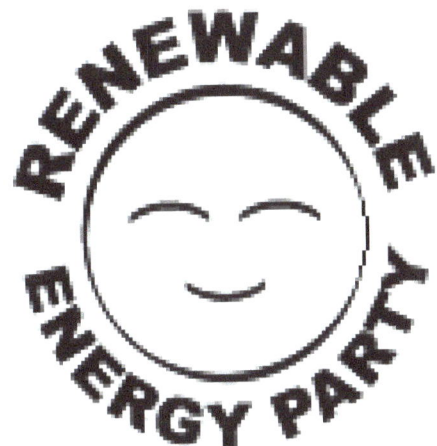

Duncan Fine's arguments against corporal punishment WEAK ! Age June 8th.

Since the complete ban nationally against corporal punishment in secondary schools we have seen an INCREASE in juvenile crime and the necessity of building more Juvenile Detention Centres.

Referencing American studies doesn't help either where 16000 deaths occur each year from 'gun violence'. He tries to confuse 'smacking' with 'violence' and 'adult cruelty', comparing family values with Dickensian workhouse cruelty. Trying to bring in laws interferring with family discipline may lead to social apartheid!

49 COUNTRIES MAKING WAR AGAINST AUSTRALIA BY DUMPING MASSIVE AMOUNTS OF DRUGS ON US

 **DP**

BEST SOLUTION FOR CAPTURED MR BIG OF DRUG IMPORTATION & DRUG MANUFACTURE

WHEN WILL NSW COPS STOP SHOOTING DEAD MEMBERS OF THE PUBLIC?

TAKE AWAY THEIR GUNS NOW!

longership.com
gunsoffcops   by tom law

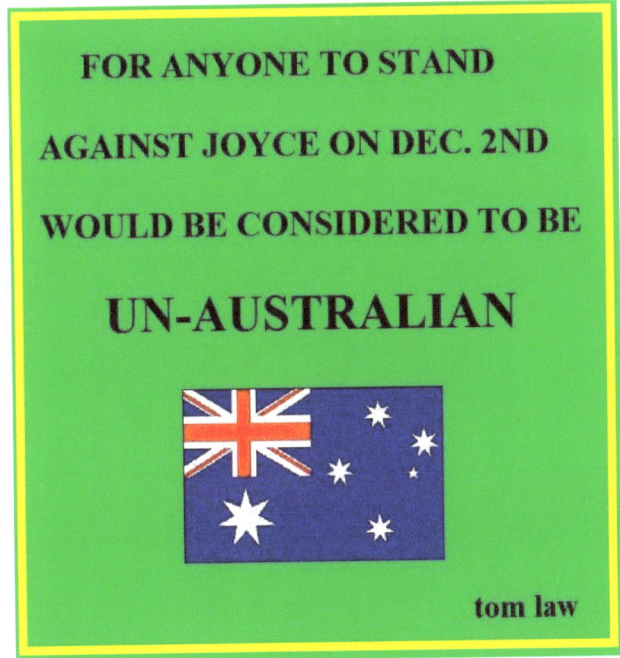

DUAL CITIZENSHIP OF AUSTRALIAN CITIZENS

IF A CITIZEN OF AUSTRALIA WAS BORN IN AUSTRALIA OR WAS ORDAINED AS A CITIZEN OF AUSTRALIA DUE TO HIS OR HER PARENTAGE THEN THAT CITIZEN CAN ONLY BE CONSIDERED TO POSSESS DUAL CITIZENSHIP ON CONDITION THAT THE FOREIGN CITIZENSHIP HAS BEEN FORMALY APPLIED FOR AND GRANTED. A FOREIGN GOVERNMENT CANNOT INSIST THAT AN AUSTRALIAN BORN CITIZEN IS A CITIZEN OF ITS COUNTRY UNLESS SUCH AN APPLICATION HAS BEEN FORMALY SUBMITTED AND CONSIDERED BY THE FOREIGN COUNTRY. HAVING THE POTENTIAL OF CITIZENSHIP OF ANOTHER COUNTRY IS IRRELEVANT .

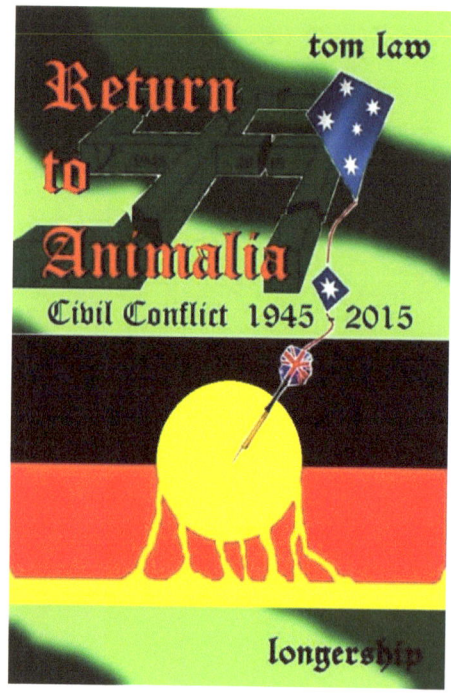

CONSPIRACY THEORISTS

"there were millions of illegal voters in the presidential elections"

"and some of the same people have killed off parts of the Great Barrier Reef!"

ANOTHER
ACT OF WAR !

AFP and Vic Police uncover

900 Kg of Methylampetamine

... reinstate DP now !!

SYMBOL OF AUSTRALIAN NATION 　　SYMBOL OF ABORIGINAL NATION
CELEBRATION DATE: 26TH JANUARY　CELEBRATION DATE:　　??

TWO NATIONS ONE LAND MASS

RECOGNITION IN THE CONSTITUTION MIGHT BRING ABOUT A CELEBRATION DATE FOR THE ABORIGINAL NATION ?

INJECTING ROOMS SAVES HEROINE ADDICTS... TRUE!

BUT THEY THEN CONTINUE TO FEED THEAT DEALERS AND FURTHER SUSTAIN THE PROBLEM!

ZERO TOLERANCE

why not?

some deserve no less!

BRITISHMANHOOD

DP FOR DRUG DEALERS !

- PROTECTING FUTURE GENERATIONS

EXPULSIONS AND RUINED LIVES

6800 kids kicked out of state schools in Victoria alone per year ? Ratio 4 boys : 1 girl

I want to know their ethnicity and religion!

Perhaps we need a **CLASS ACTION** against the Government with monetary compensation !

* reintroduction of corporal punishment OR kids living on the street and /or into Detention Centres? .. SAVE THE KIDS!

BRITISHMANHOOD

.. plus more police powers to hold kids of 14 years for up to 36 hours !!

DEATH PENALTY REVISITED

SARAH GILL ARTICLE, THE AGE MAY 4TH, PERHAPS COMES FROM HER HEART BUT IGNORES THE TRUTH: "AUSTRALIA IS NOW IN A CONSTANT STATE OF WAR FROM BOTH EXTERNAL AND INTERNAL PARTICIPANTS"

ACTS OF WAR

IMPORTATION AND LOCAL MANUFACTURE AND DISTRIBUTION OF DRUGS THAT ARE "KILLING OUR SOCIETY, TEARING APART SOCIAL FABRIC!"

RELEASE OF MURDERERS THAT THEN GO ON TO RECOMMIT

AUSTRALIANS INDIRECTLY SUPPORT THE DEATH PENALTY BY PERMITTING THOUSANDS TO DIE FROM DRUG OVERDOSE AS WELL AS POLICE SHOOTING CRIMINALS DEAD ON SIGHT!

COCAINE ICE HEROINE LSD AND MANY NEWBIES FROM EASTERN EUROPE, ASIA AND SOUTH AMERICA ARRIVING NOW BY THE CONTAINER LOAD !!

... read 'Return to Animalia' by Tom Law

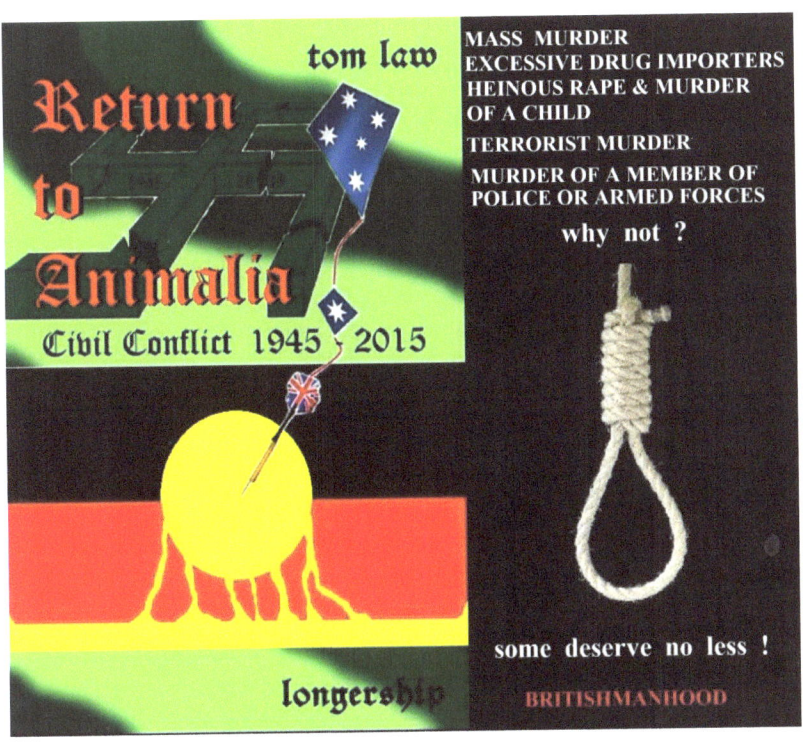

PARADISE NEWS

Est. 1885

Sunday
5th November 2017

DEARTH IN PARADISE !

It seems that all is not well in Paradise with the news that it has been reported that there is a DEARTH of TAX being paid by the Super Rich and many of the Global Enterprises in the country!

A well known lawyer in the city was quoted today saying: " It is not an illegal practice.. and has been going on for quite some time now."

A Government spokesperson from the Tax Dept. said it was most immoral and costing the country billions of dollars in lost revenue .. basically they are tax cheats.. but what else would you expect from those at the top of the pile ?

An unemployed vagrant one Joe Blow in the street when asked his opinion succinctly replied: "I'd stand the buggars against a wall and shoot the lot of 'em ! "

Reporters: Hazel Moneypenny & Dan Appleby

TIME TO STEP IN

GG

NEEDS TO DISSOLVE BOTH HOUSES AND CALL FOR FRESH ELECTIONS TO SOLVE PROBLEM OF DUAL CITIZENSHIP DEBACLE !!

November 2017

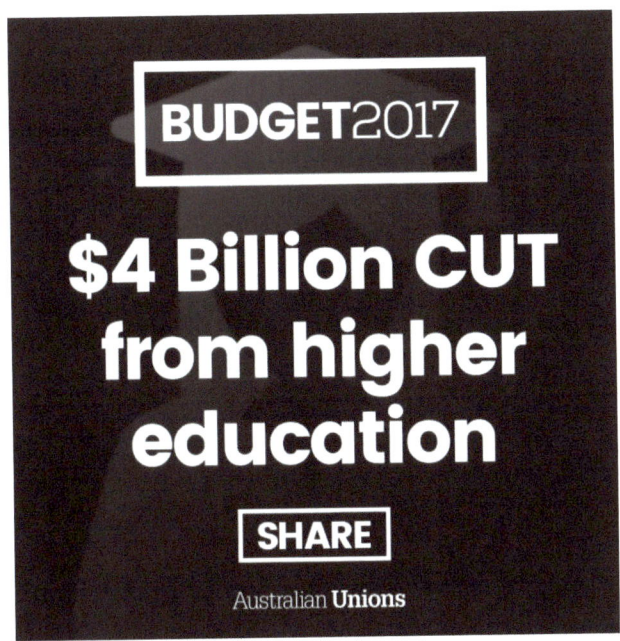

Retweet

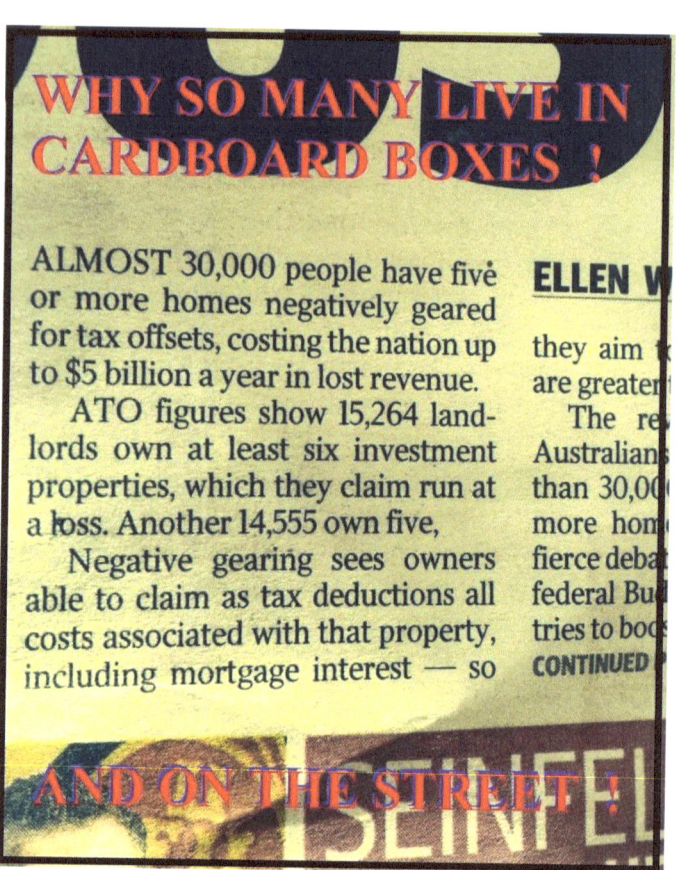

OUR NED FIRST MUSLIM TERRORIST ?

the burka

the beard

.. and definitely no respect for judges ..
a true Australian !!

"If these people want to come to live here, respect our laws. Even in courtrooms, they have no respect for the judges, won't even stand up. I think the burka should absolutely go. This is, you know, it's Australia. The full face covering, I think is wrong. If they want to live that way and have their law, Sharia law and all the rest of it, I suggest go to a Muslim country."

Pauline Pantsdown

Retweet

Pauline Handsome demurely sits in the Senate!

Lost in Paradise? .. its O-Cay-Man !!

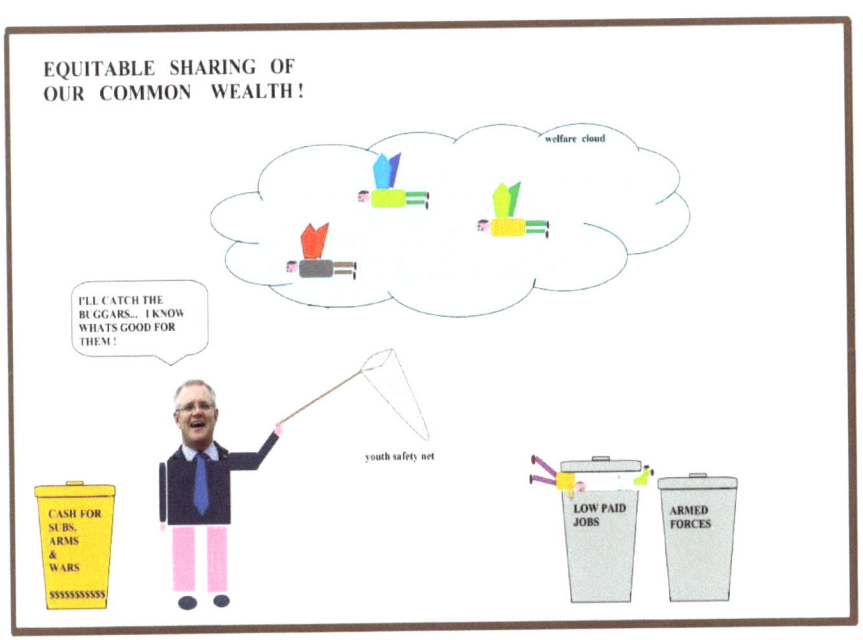

The lone ranger

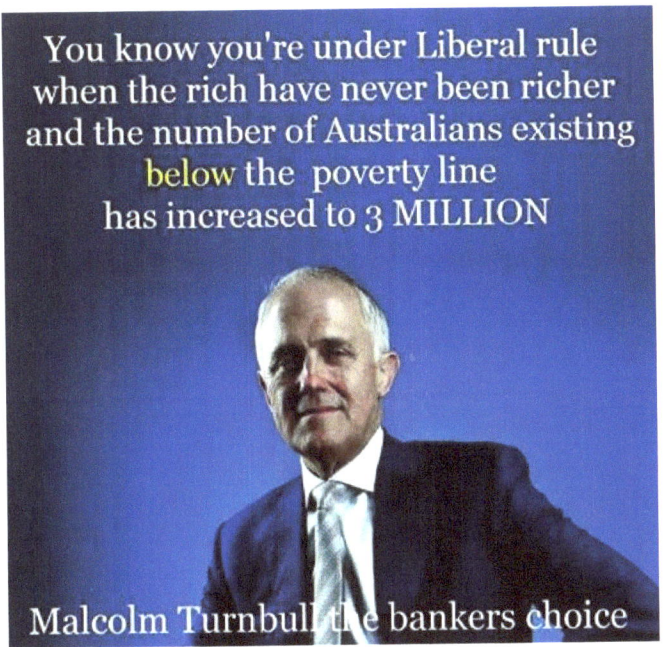

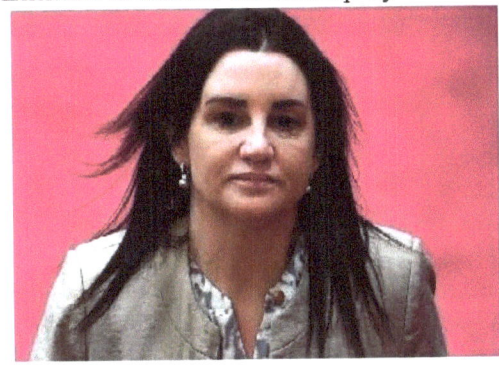

II   *America*

If you view my tweets regarding America you might have the misconception that I wish to constantly attack that country! But it is not the case.. this is supposed to be a light hearted affair, highlighting some of the more pertinent goings on over the past twelve months and not least of all the eruptions and shenanigans surrounding the Presidency. The 'Russian thingi' never went away. Heads have rolled in the White House. White Supremacists have raised their ugly voices and terrorism of a home grown kind as well as the Islamic kind have joined the horrendous statistics of gun deaths in America due to stupid gun laws and the 2nd Amendment! We point to some of these not merely as a critic but also as a friend! Besides these laws and the strength of the NRA it is disturbing to see the enormous contracts for armaments by American companies supplying Israel, Saudi Arabia and many other nations. But America is not alone in this despicable business bringing the world ever closer to its finale! The human suffering due to wars across the globe is outrageous and those that trade in arms have a lot to answer for! Then there are those smaller nations wishing to join the exclusive 'Nuclear Club'. Despite all the hypocrisy, sorry.. but it is just not permitted and there are likely to be consequences! Iran and North Korea are the current naughty boys deserving a spanking! It is a tragedy that money is more important than sensible action when it comes to things like the environment, gun laws and Bank profits. Over the year America has experienced both good and bad fortune.. progress on its space exploration program, an improvement on its economic development but with forest fires, devastating hurricanes and loony terrorists! Will 'The Wall' ever be built? Will Obama Care ever be stripped? Will harmonious relations with China persist? These are all questions whose answers we will have to wait patiently to realise!

freedom of speech ??

AMERICAN FREEDOM DEFENSE INITIATIVE

NO ! ... freedom to express
HATRED !!

DEREGULATE AND PROSECUTE HATE INCITING ORGANISATIONS NOW !

AMERICA
IS A GREAT COUNTRY

FOR ALL !!

DEMOCRACY IN ACTION

TRUMP   59,135,740
CLINTON 59,299,381

We declare 'TRUMP' the winner !

America's finest !

are not the wild west days far behind?

'guns off cops guns off everyone'
by tom law
amazon.com

ARYAN NATIONS ...

... you cannot get rid of this scum by polite discussion and peaceful demonstration !!

ALL COPS AREN'T BAD, ALL AFRO AMERICANS AREN'T THUGS, ALL WHITES AREN'T RACIST

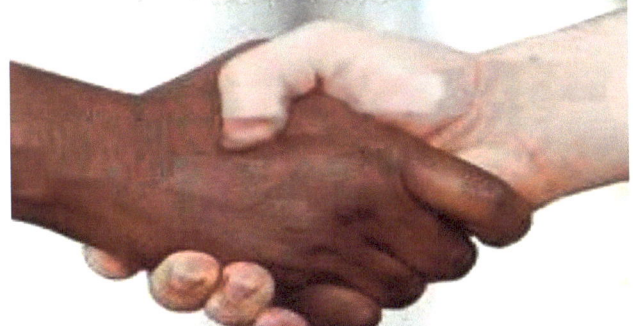

IF WE COME TOGETHER AND UNITE AS ONE WE CAN BE AN UNSTOPPABLE FORCE

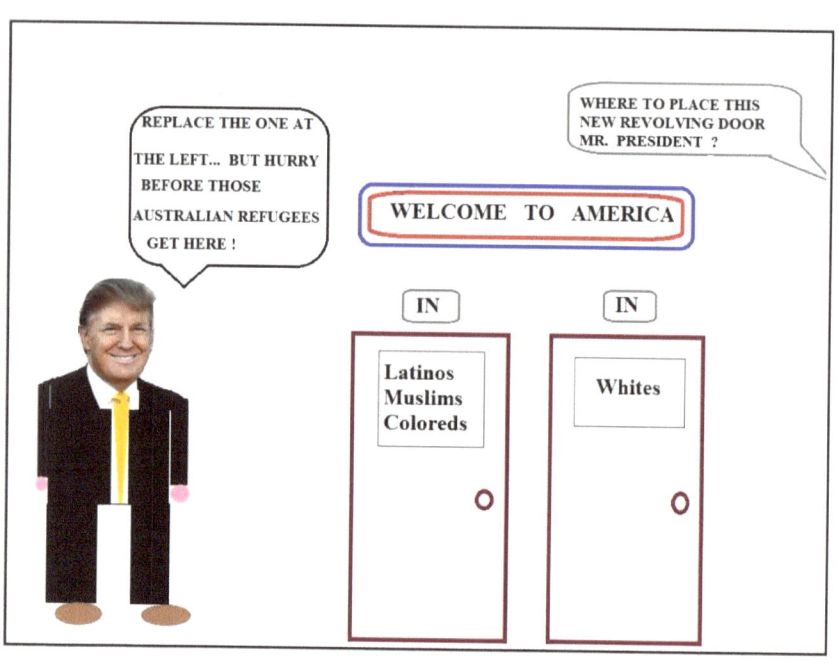
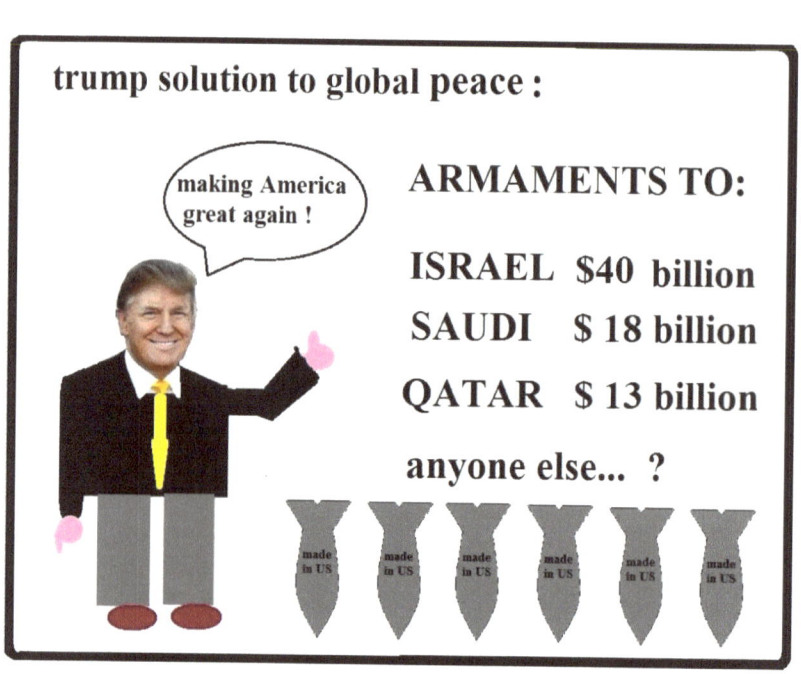

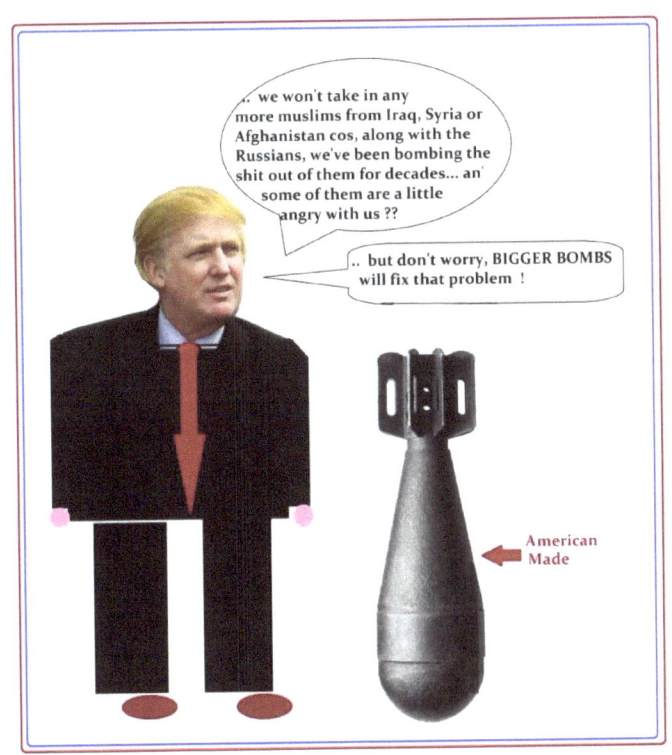

Allah is Satan ?? .. I think he meant to say "Allah is Great!"

$150 Billion Armaments Deal

to a country that:
beheads criminals by the sword
has no rights for women
commits war crimes against neighbours
has provided cash to ISIS

BUT Donald Trump   doesn't care one iota !

THIS IS THE BUSINESS OF ETERNAL WAR
THIS IS THE BUSINESS OF MURDER
THIS IS AMERICA'S MONEY SPINNER

WHAT ELSE TO DO

WITH AN INSECT ?

NORTH KOREA USED SOME RADIATIVE WEAPON ON "Otto Warmbier" ... PROBABLY A COLD MICROWAVE MASER. THIS SEEMS TO BE AN ACT OF WAR DEMANDING A RESPONSE !!

Tom Law's analysis

DONALDS NEW FAVOURITE FRUIT ?

Retweet

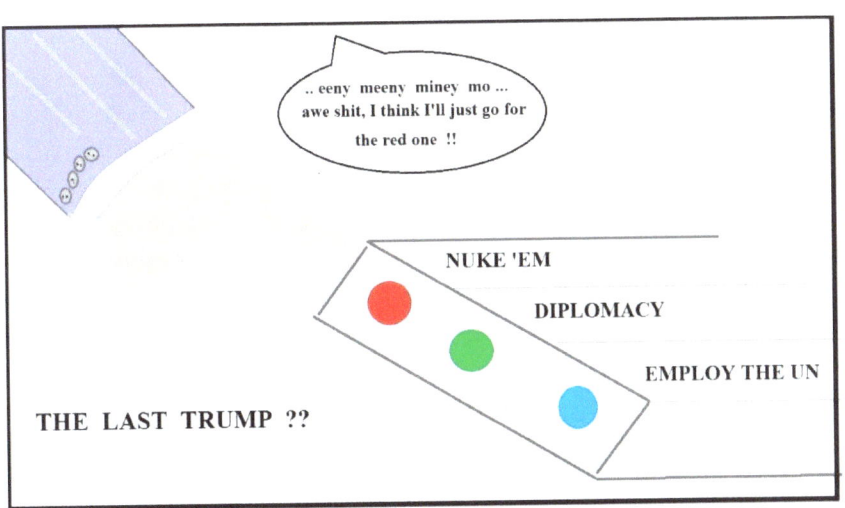

FIRST 100 DAYS

I decree:
- burn more coal
- make bigger bombs
- pay more for medical
- manufacture more guns

gunsoffcops.com

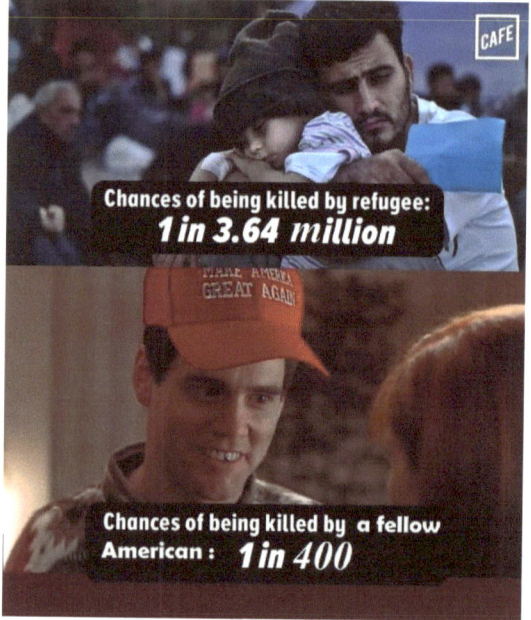

Taking your chances!

SOME HELPFUL ADVICE TO EVERYTOWN FROM BETSY RIOT:

DON'T HOLD HANDS WITH FASCISTS.

Retweet from BetsyRiot..   don't ya just luv her !!

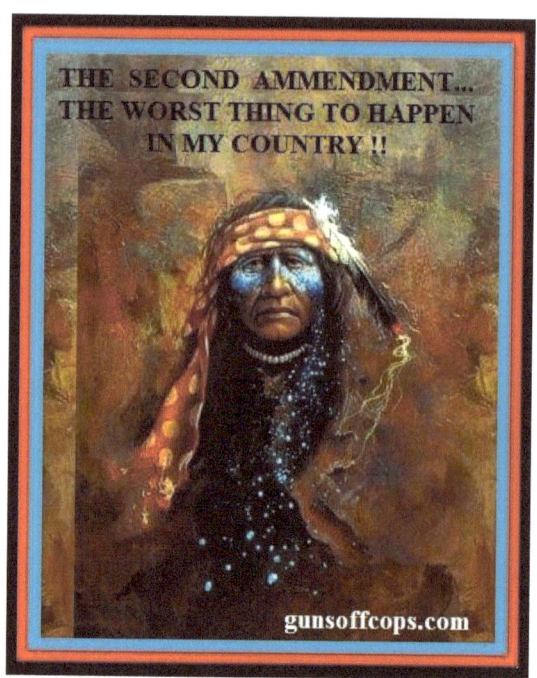

THE SECOND AMMENDMENT...
THE WORST THING TO HAPPEN
IN MY COUNTRY !!

gunsoffcops.com

THE LAST TRUMP

MORE NUKES FOR US

.. and to hell with poverty and all our other problems !

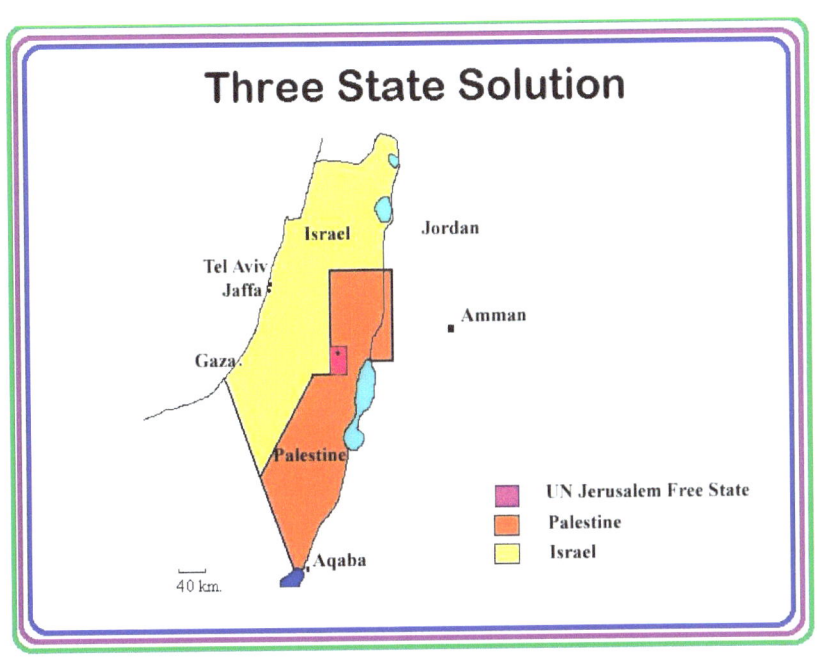

Despite the continual carnage, gun sales have never been higher !

"A hard rain's gonna fly IN EVERY DIRECTION !"

Definitely!

 **Donald J. Trump** @realDonaldTrump · 1h
Do you notice we are not having a gun debate right now? That's because they used knives and a truck!

And what do you think would have happened if they had the same access to guns in England as they do here genius? It's like he's trying to poison us with hypocrisy and irony. Thank a Republican for putting an imbecile in charge so he could befriend our enemies and alienate our allies.

AMERICAN NEWSX

Retweets

Retweets

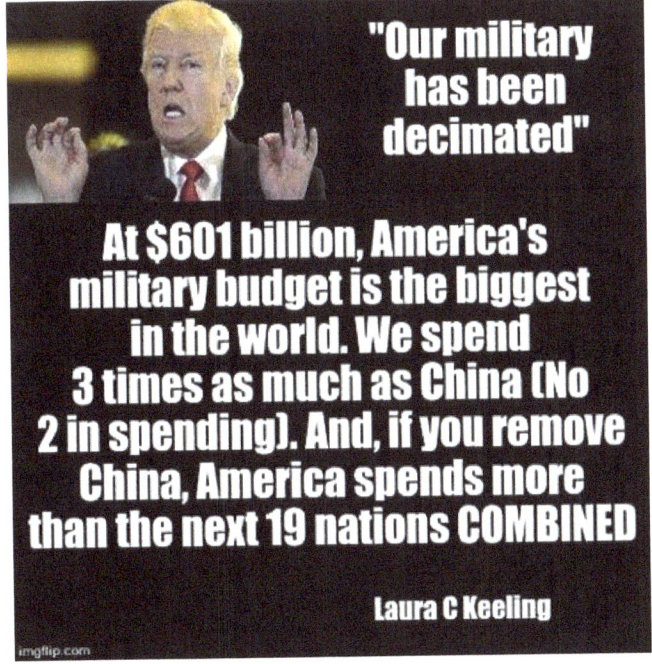

National Gun Violence Awareness Day   June 2 2017

Retweets

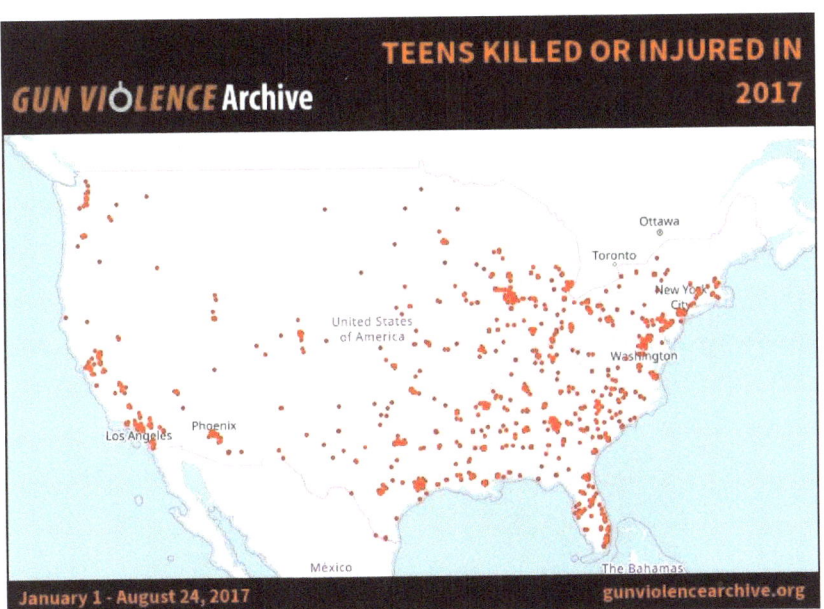

Real meaning of the 2nd Amendment !

… an' teenage girls ? … or so I bin told !!

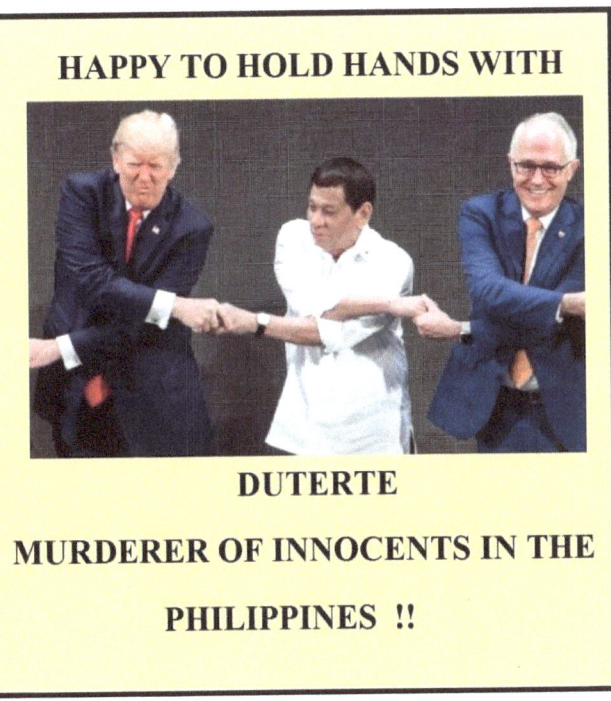

HAPPY TO HOLD HANDS WITH DUTERTE MURDERER OF INNOCENTS IN THE PHILIPPINES !!

Recorded for all of time ! Disgraceful !!

Based on tweet by betsyriot

III   *Britain*

I think I am a lone voice in stating that I believe Russia interfered in the 2014 parliamentary elections, the Scottish Referendum on Independence and on the Brexit plebiscite! But then again it might have been by some other nation or a collection of nations? Paranoia you declare? Maybe! But it seems that there is also a 'Make Britain Great Again' feeling in the country by many but whether Brexit will bring it about remains to be seen! As in America and France, Britain has suffered its share of Islamic terrorism over the last year. But let us not forget our self-righteous involvement in wars in the Middle East and Afghanistan. It seems self evident that if a nation joins a war (for whatever reason) there is always likely to be some cost and retaliation. Tom doesn't think all is as simple as the polies and media dish out to us! Her Majesty is still soldiering on but her partner Prince Philip duly retired after a very long period in service of the country. The wankers in the English defence League continue to be a festering sore and blight on the nation. Aluminium has proven itself to be as dangerous as rocket fuel in the building industry. Our international armaments industries have about as much morality as their 'brothers in arms' in America, France, Russia, China and so many other countries making money and sustaining high profits at the cost of global destruction and human suffering on an unprecedented scale. I was so incensed over this state of affairs I just had to write my new book titled "Helter Skelter" predicting the final abyss and demise of all the great civilisations of the world through greed and total apathy of people ignoring 'all the signs'. Despite being a nation that has shown leadership in the world it has not been forceful enough in bringing Israel to heel and permitting Palestinian emancipation and nationhood. As a prime mover of the creation of Israel, is it not time to assist the Palestinians?

INTERFERENCE IN:

✦ 2014 GENERAL ELECTION

✦ SCOTTISH REFERENDUM

✦ BREXIT REFERENDUM

WHAT NEXT ?

DISASTER EMERGANCY COMMITTEE

HAPPY RETIREMENT PRINCE PHILIP !

70 years of service

THE QUESTION IS ON RIGHTS

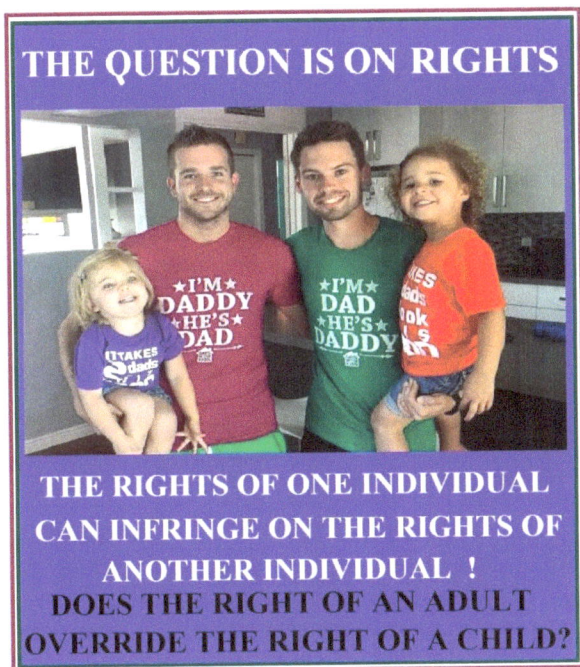

THE RIGHTS OF ONE INDIVIDUAL CAN INFRINGE ON THE RIGHTS OF ANOTHER INDIVIDUAL !
DOES THE RIGHT OF AN ADULT OVERRIDE THE RIGHT OF A CHILD?

Children have a RIGHT to a mum and a dad !

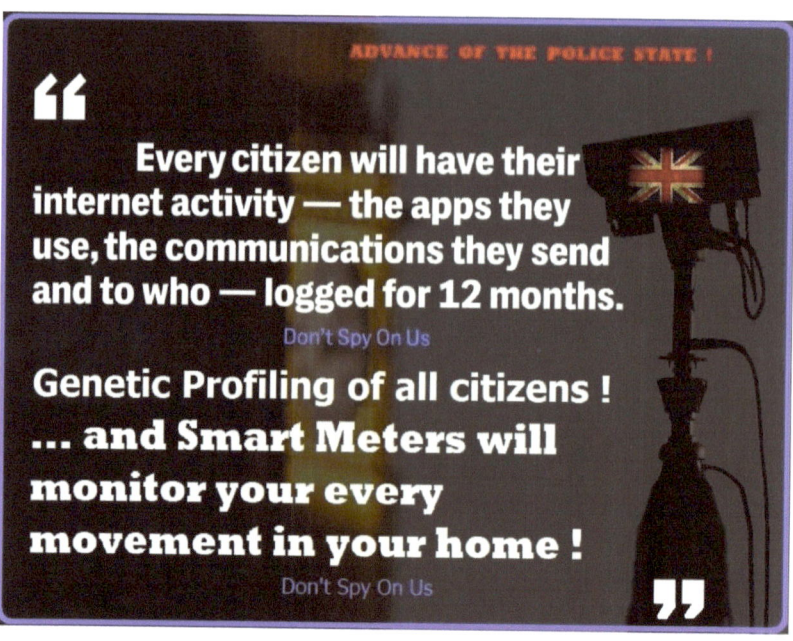

BRAK BREXIT
NOW

BREXIT ??

NEIN !!

Go with Scottish Labour the way forward

LESSON OF ALUMINIUM

AS WITH THE HMS SHEFFIELD IN THE FALKLANDS WAR THE FIRE AT GRENFELL TOWER OWES ITS FEROCITY TO THE PRESENCE OF ALUMINIUM !

ALUMINIUM DOES NOT IGNITE EASILY, BUT ONCE BURNING, IT IS AKIN TO ROCKET FUEL AND CANNOT BE EASILY EXTINGUISHED !

... A TERRIBLE TRAGEDY !!

TO BE AGAINST ISRAELI GOVT. POLICY IS NOT TO BE CONFUSED

Leaders' election pledges to *Jewish News* readers

- ✓ Zero-tolerance on anti-Semitism
- ✓ Proudly stand up for Israel
- ✓ Protect Jewish schools and shuls
- ✓ Safeguard shechita
- ✓ Boost trade with Israel

After two years, he *still* hasn't spoken to us

Full election coverage on pages 3, 4, 6, 8, 9, 16 & 19

WITH ANTISEMITISM.. THEY'RE COMPLETELY DIFFERENT !!

This is Nob.

Nob is working class but votes Tory because the newspapers tell him to.

After the tories get into power they screw working class voters like Nob and give the newspaper owners massive tax cuts.

Dont be a Nob.

Dont vote tory.

**DON'T BE A NOB !!
DONT VOTE TORY !!**

2000 DAYS IN JAIL FOR HIS HUMAN RIGHTS WORK

Human rights lawyer Abdolfattah Soltani has been jailed since 2011. He is serving a 13-year prison sentence.

#FreeSoltani

IRAN: END HIS UNJUST IMPRISONMENT NOW

.. and the BEST of friends !!

did these men choreograph

these video clips… and more?

MASTERS OF THE DARK ARTS

BELL & POTTINGER
of
LONDON
"we can make you believe ANYTHING !"

Masters of the 'Dark Arts' .. propaganda and persuasion !

"Get out of our English Channel !!"

GRENFELL & FINSBURY

HAVE THE AUTHORITIES LIED TO THE BRITISH PEOPLE ? WERE THESE BOTH ATTACKS ON BRITISH MUSLIMS BY THE EXTREME RIGHT?

A question !

ARMAMENTS AND WEAPONS MANUFACTURE AND SALES

BY YOUR GREEDY COUNTRY IS DESTROYING THE WORLD

IF BREXIT WAS A CONSTITUTIONAL CHANGE

THEN POLL REQUIRED 67% FOR SUCCESS!

CAMERON'S FAULT FOR NOT APPLYING

SENSIBLE RULES. WILL WE HAVE FUTURE

REFERENDUMS BASED ON WHIMS ???

Hitler also scoffed and laughed at us Mr Putin !!

Song: 'RADIO STAR DIANA' by Chas Rose 1998
Devoted to the 'Peoples Princess'

… and to be found on Youtube !

British nuclear weapon transport entering Glencorse barracks in Penicuik today. If loaded this truck will be carrying a warhead containing both high explosive and plutonium. The consequences of an accident could be catastrophic. The purpose of the weapons is mass incineration. This is Scotland 2017

Retweet

Retweets

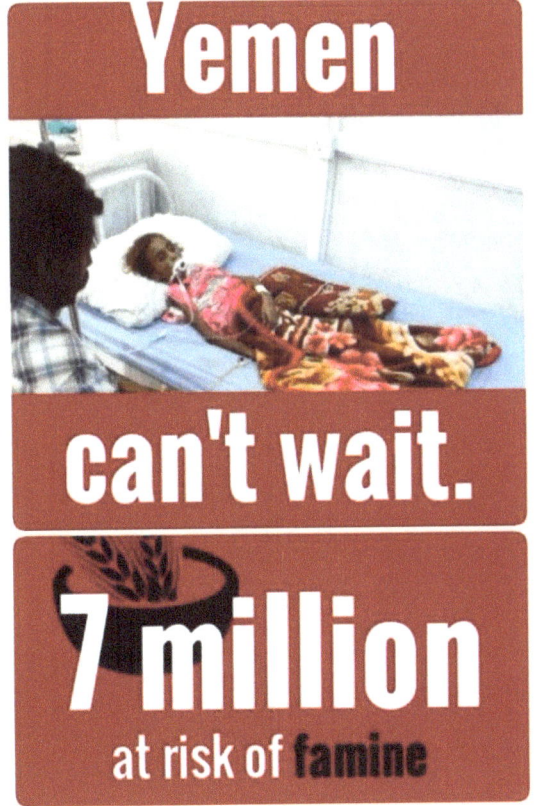

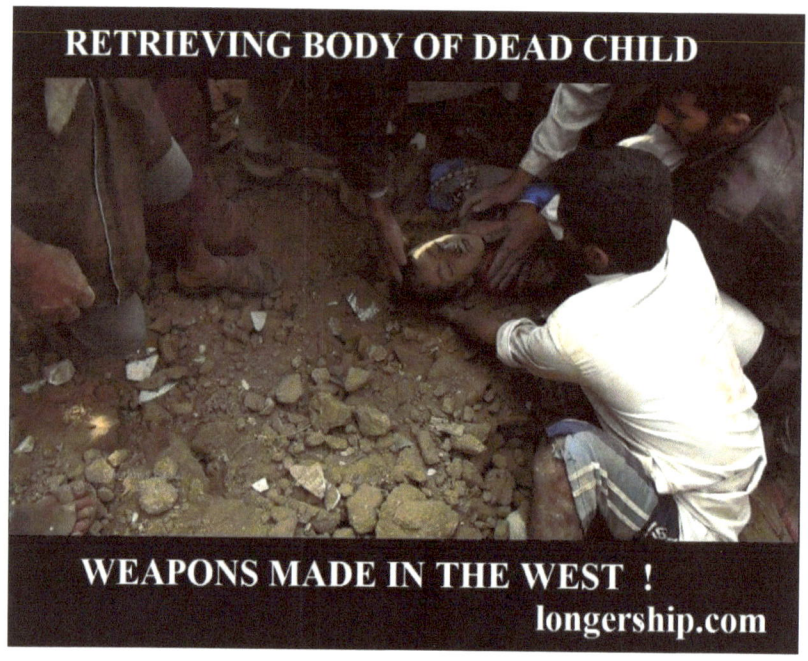

IV   Wars

I know it may be construed as a cynical remark but there are two basic premises one can say about wars, namely:

(i)   War is nearly always about money

(ii)   The first casualty of war is 'the truth'

We have seen in the past 'The War to End Wars' and other gems such as 'It Will All Be Over By Christmas'.. but it never is. As I have said, we live in a failed world when it comes to ending wars between nations. Even with those hideous terrorist groups that wish to make war, there is still a need and requirement of weapons, ammunition and chemical supplies to keep it going. And there is also a need for a great money supply to pay for it all. Sadly, this never seems to be problematic.. money can always be found to procure the tools to make war! Armaments manufacturers and salespersons have a big responsibility to the peoples of the world generally. Unfortunately their responsibilities seem to lie more importantly with shareholders that scream for profit and dividends on their investment! There are many wars going on around the world with the greatest numbers of deaths, destruction and refugees ever seen.. some eighty million at present. Whilst not totally sterile, the United Nations does not seem to function quite as it should to eliminate war. Perhaps there is a problem with its structure, particularly the permanency of some giants in the Security Council and their ridiculous power of Veto over important decision making! It is this impediment that makes it currently almost impossible to rid the world of Nuclear Weapons and other weapons of mass destruction. The giants also depend on sales of weapons and military hardware to maintain their national high standards of living. This is Capitalism gone Mad! Even Colonel Custer had to fight the American Indians that had purchased rifles from gun retailers!

Retweet   Scary BUT clever! - adopted by Hitler to go into Poland !

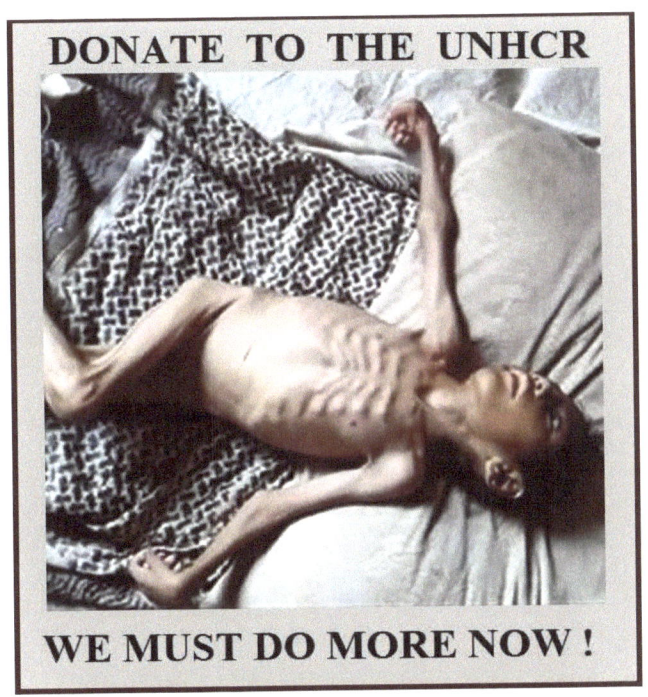

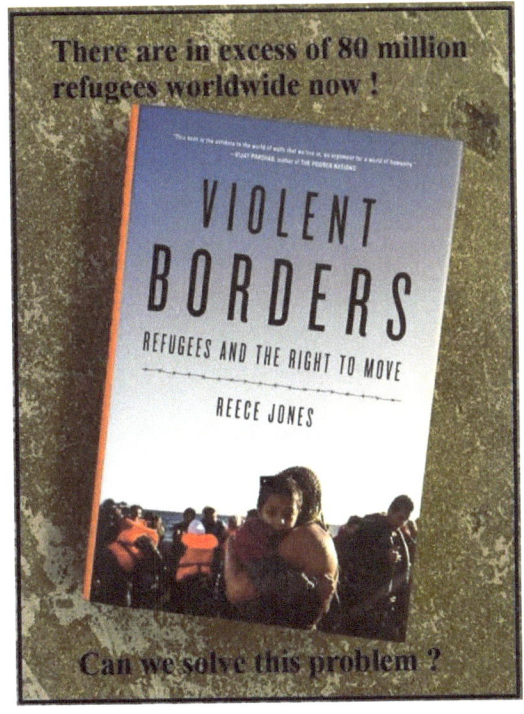

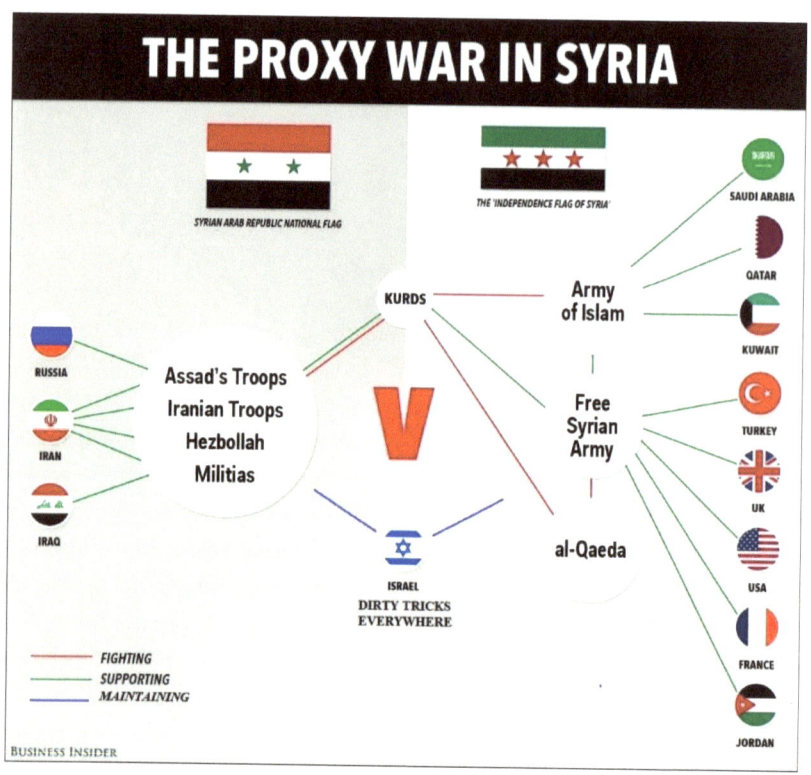

Retweet

The finality of humanity on this planet!   Available at: amazon.com

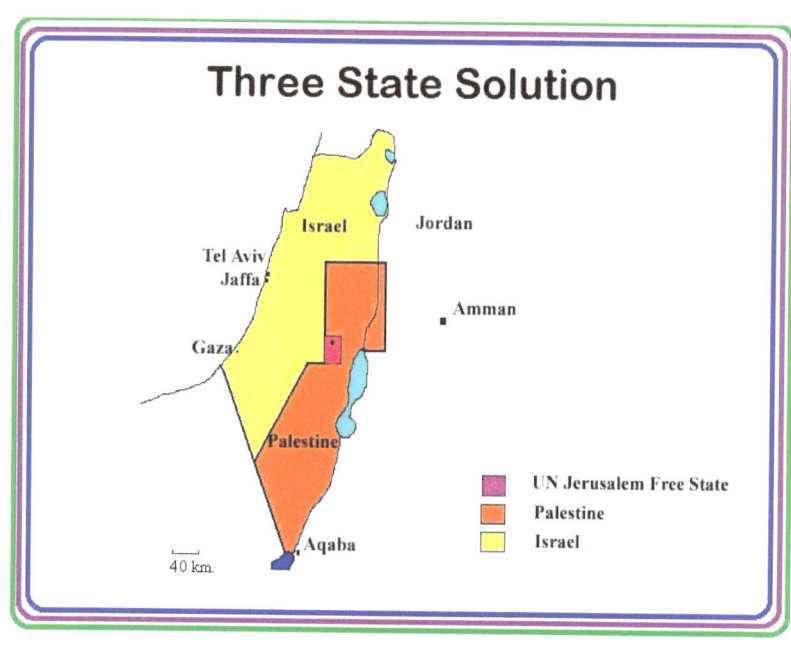

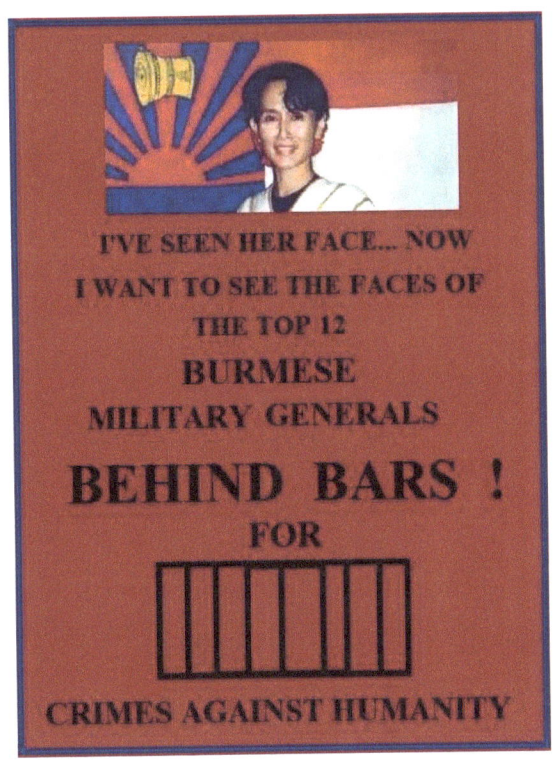

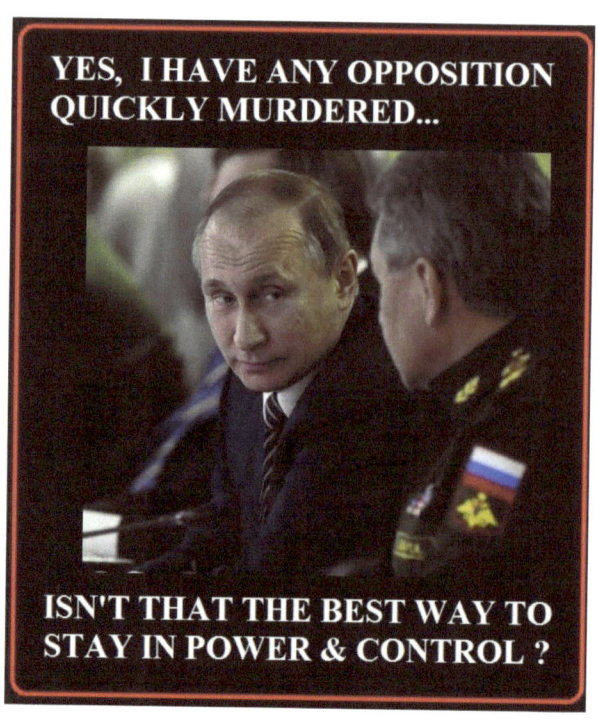

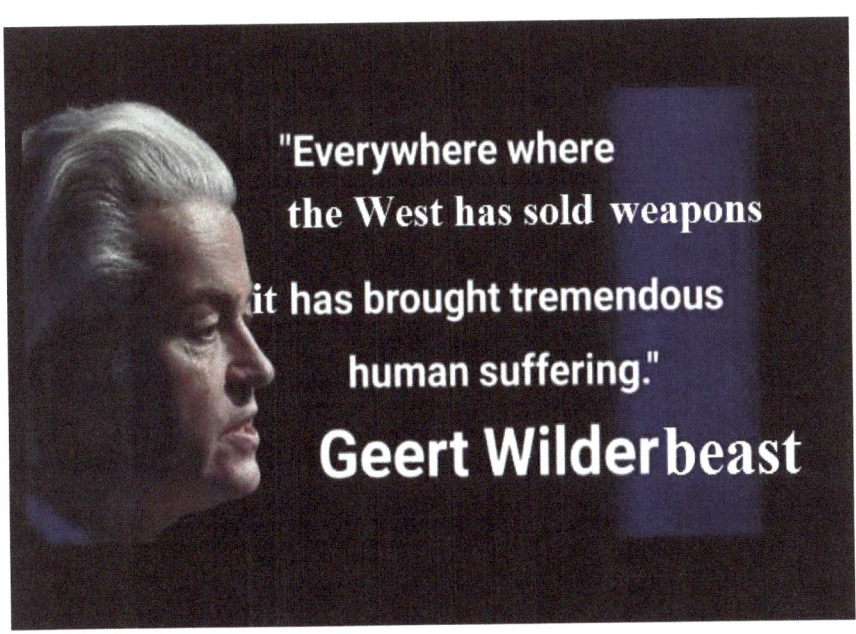

MAYBE TRUMP'S INVESTMENTS IN INDONESIA GONE DOWN DRAIN ??

Indonesian Armed Forces Chief General Gatot Nurmantyo had been invited to a countering violent extremism conference in Washington. **BUT DENIED ENTRY TO US!**

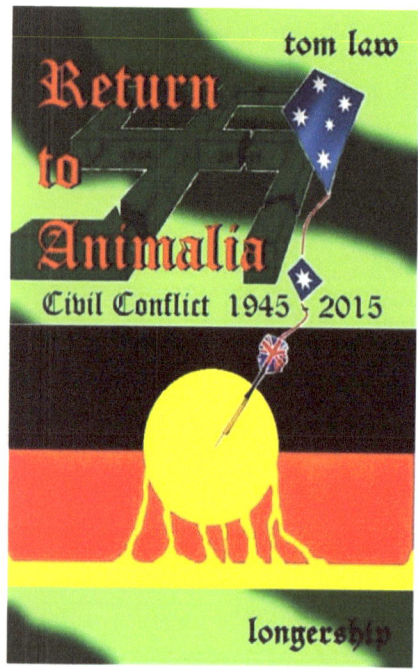

.. a disgrace that all this is happening in the 21st Century !!

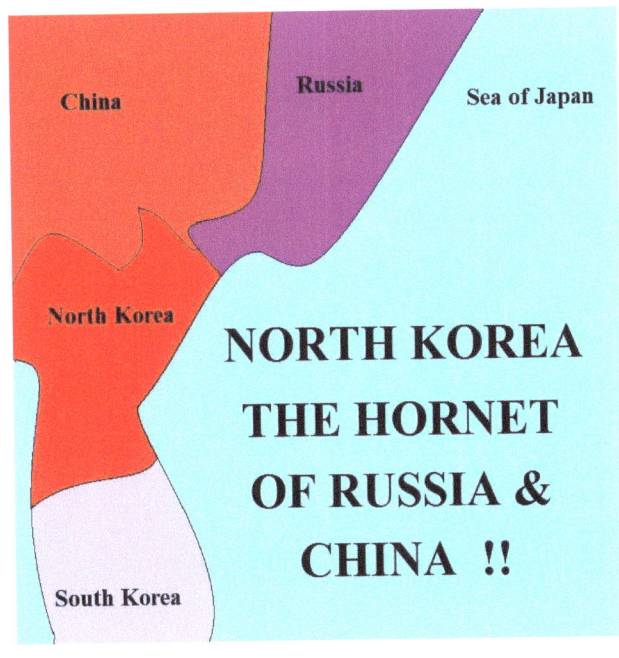

I ALWAYS THOUGHT THAT BUDDHISM WAS A PEACEFUL RELIGION ?
... I WAS WRONG !

DESPITE DEMOCRACY, MYANMAR'S MILITARY COMMITING GENOCIDE TO MINORITY GROUP !

THIS CAN ONLY COURT RETRIBUTION AND VIOLENCE AT A LATER TIME !

CHINA DID NOTHING WITH NORTH KOREA...

... THIS IS WHAT THE EARTH LOOKS LIKE NOW !!

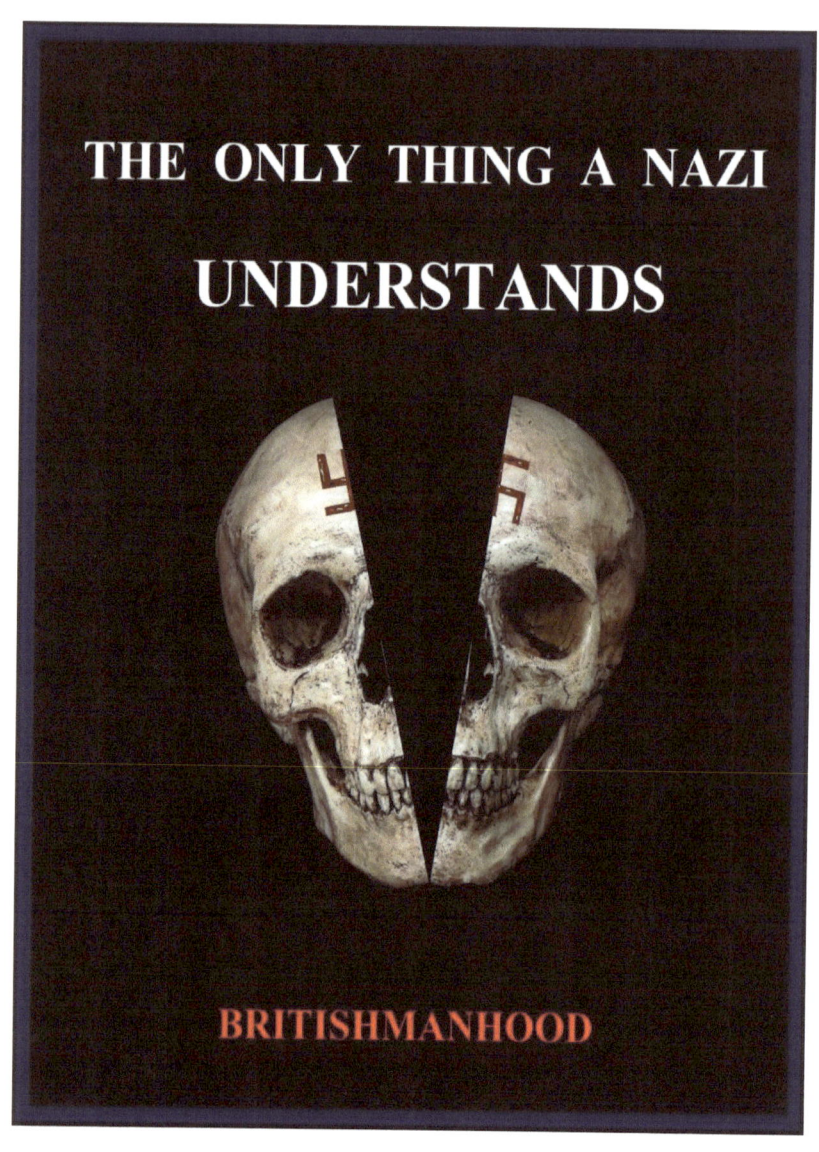

Ramadan ... pity IS and Sunni extremists have thrown

away the true meaning of "peace and good will" to all ! SHAME

Adapted from tweet from @TomthunkitsMind

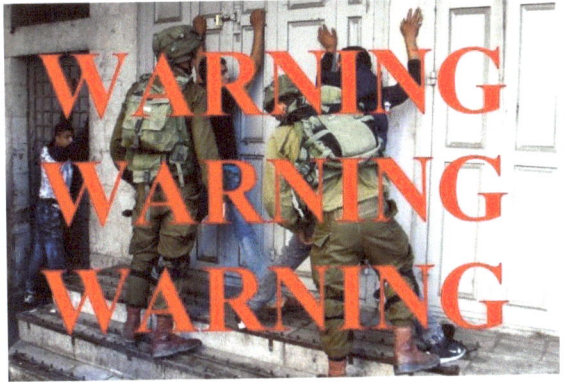

COMPULSORY ARMBAND FOR WHITE SUPREMACISTS

'untermensch'

... let them wear it for 5 years... the length of WWII

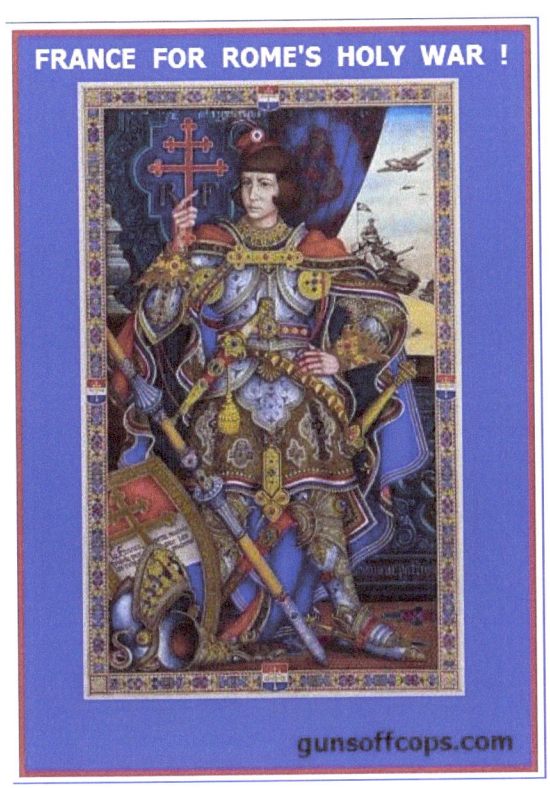

Are you ready comrade ?

Also known as 'Rocket Man' !!

RUSSIAN ATTEMPTS TO THEORISE ON SYRIAN GAS ATTACKS POINTS TO THEIR

COMPLICITY

AFTER ALL, THE RUSSIAN MILITARY USED CHEMICAL ATTACKS IN AFGHANISTAN BETWEEN 1979 AND 1982 MORE THAN FORTY TIMES !!

UN SYRIA DISARMING FORCE

ALL NATIONS TO CONTRIBUTE ARMED PERSONNEL AND/OR POLICE EQUIVALENT TO 0.01 % OF THEIR POPULATION WITH THE EXCEPTIONS OF ISRAEL/PALESTINE AND THOSE NATIONS DEEMED TO BE FAILED STATES.

SYRIA NOW DEEMED TO BE A COLLAPSED SOCIETY !

CAN ONLY BE A UN SOLUTION !

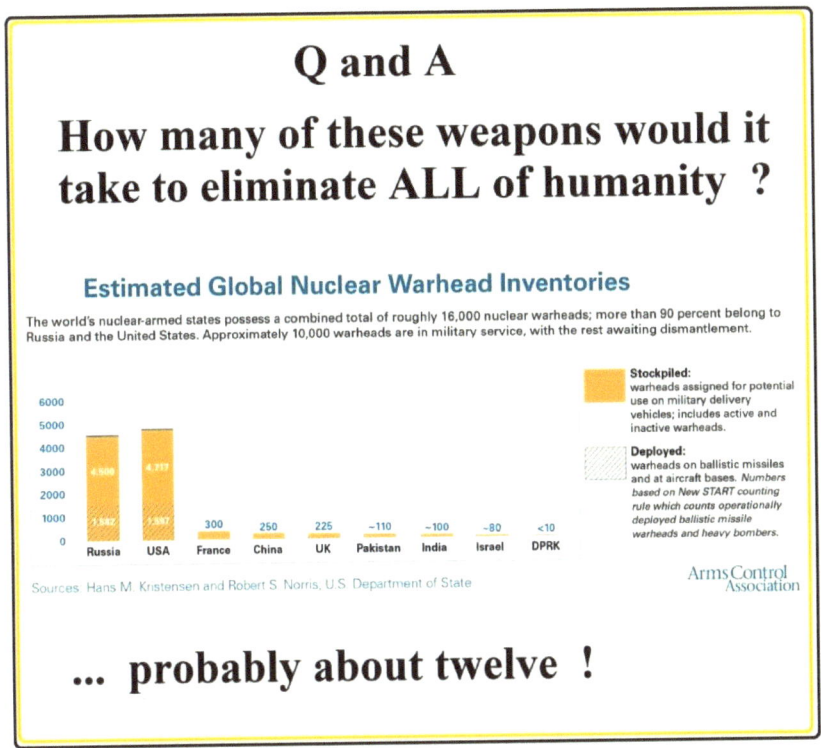

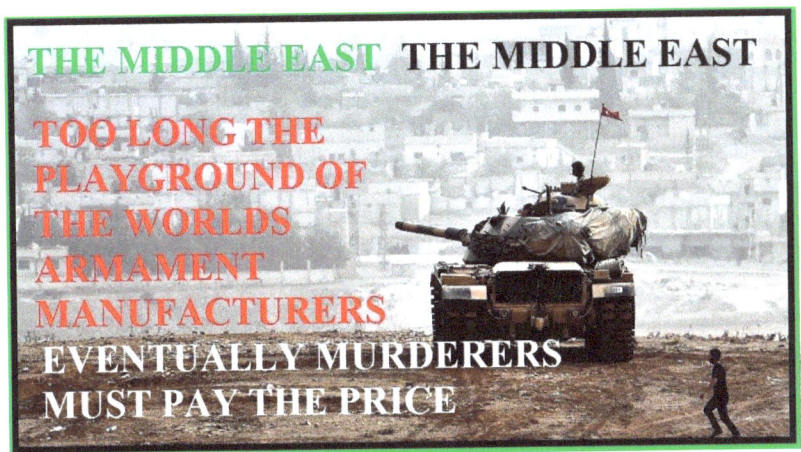

Retweet

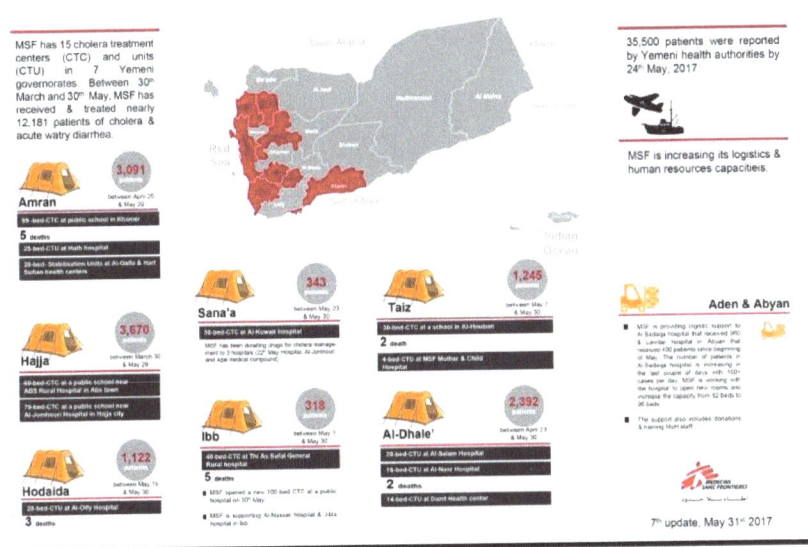

Thankyou Saudi Arabia.. one of the richest countries in the world!

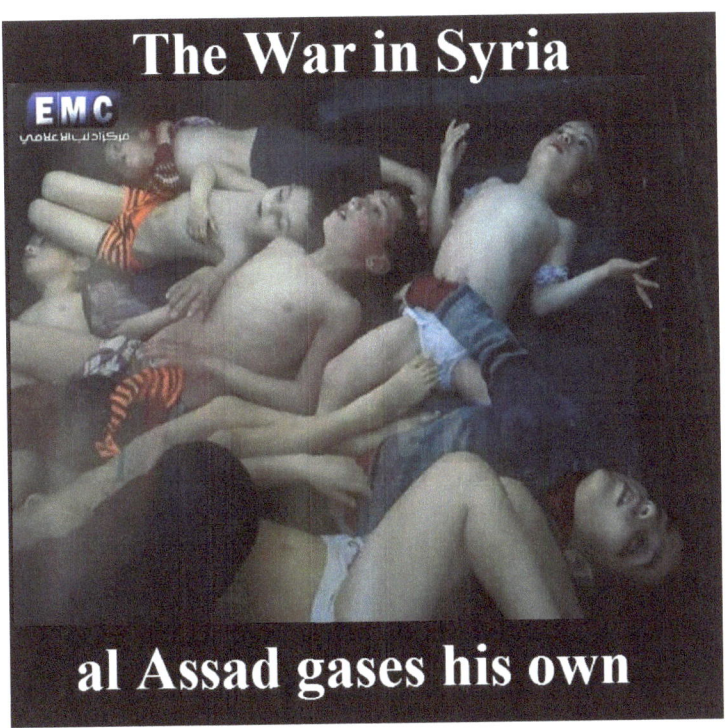

.. and I firmly believe in God, the afterlife and retribution!   TL

I just hope that one day these will not be your children..   Helter Skelter

Tom Law

KEEPING THE WORLD SAFE ?
... I THINK NOT ...   JUST BRINGING THIS TO ALL THE WORLD AND EVER CLOSER !!

Helter Skelter   by Tom Law
longership.com   amazon.com

JERUSALEM
SHOULD BELONG TO THE WHOLE WORLD,
NOT ISRAEL OR PALESTINE ALONE

UN JERUSALEM FREE STATE

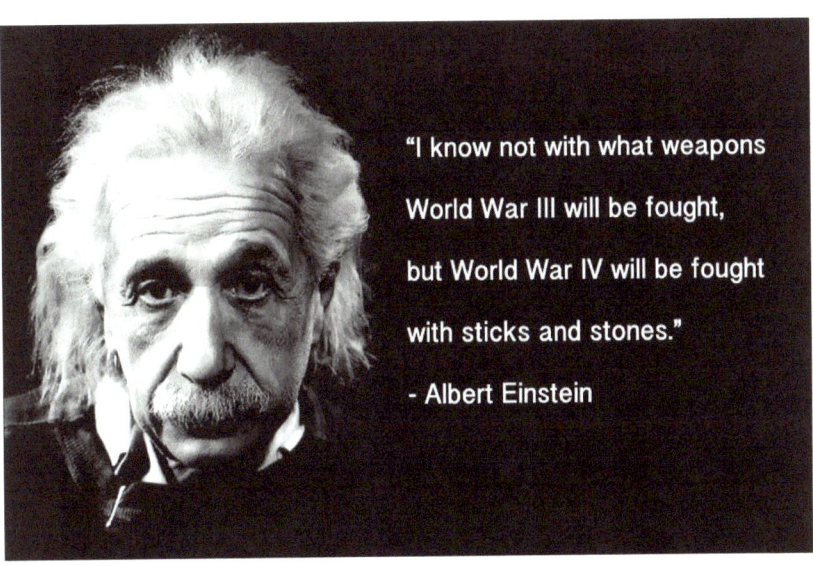

"I know not with what weapons World War III will be fought, but World War IV will be fought with sticks and stones."
- Albert Einstein

… maybe this is the future for us all ?   Read: 'Helter Skelter' by Tom Law

V *Guns*

I wrote a book titled 'Guns Off Cops, Guns Off Everyone' which was published in 2016. It was my pet concern at the time and though many would label Tom Law as being somewhat naïve, I still today think it possible to greatly reduce the number of gun deaths in the world as well as eliminate the need for wars implementing horrific killing machines. Yes, I am indeed a poet and a dreamer. I unreservedly confess this but sometimes it is the dreamers and philosophers that have contributed to the sensibilities of correct action and by small steps have brought the peoples of the world to what is described as more civilised. High civilisations are marked by high culture, tolerance, sentience and generally the avoidance of conflict as a means of resolution of disagreement between nations. Sometimes 'The Law' is an ass, however the evolution of all the various types of law and their application is to remove the possibility of violence in solving problems. Thus I continue to try to persuade people generally to think about the introduction of sensible and holistic gun laws in their country. Having lived in a rural setting for many decades I am not opposed to recreational shooting and gun ownership per se. However I do not see that an individual needs to store at home or carry on ones person a handgun. A clubhouse is the best place where they are stored under lock and key! Nor do I see the necessity of ownership of more than two or three at most firearms by one individual. National registration of licensed shooters and each and every firearm in circulation is paramount. There is no place for fully automatic or military style weapons among the general public!

Manufacturers of recreational firearms as well as the more serious military weapons have an enormous responsibility in ensuring the safety of society. Breaches of strict rules should earn most severe penalties in fines or, in the worst case, a total close down of the business!

Charlemagne

Prince James Stuart

DEAR AMERICA

TAKE NOTE OF YOUR AUSSIE MATES ...

GUN AMNESTY

FOR A SAFER SOCIETY !

... and PLEASE don't shoot at us whilst we are visiting you !!

... that's ma boy !!

... as you can see, they already shot the teachers!

longership.com   gunsoffcops

SOLVING AMERICAS PROBLEMS ?

AMMUNITION DEPOT — HUGE INVENTORY — GREAT PRICES

Most Brands and Calibers of Pistol and Rifle Ammo!

Want **LOW COST** AMMO?
Need **HIGH QUALITY** AMMO?
We offer both at
GREAT PRICES

GUNSOFFCOPS.COM

I Carry A Gun
NOT BUT BECAUSE
BECAUSE I'm Scared and
IT'S A my IQ is < 85 !
WEAPON

URBAN CARRY MORONS
www.UrbanCarryMorons.com

VI *Climate & Environment*

It has been scientifically proven beyond doubt that the industrial age of the last two to three hundred years has had an effect on the planet's climate and that the current explosion of developing countries hindered by the demands of huge populations is bringing the world to a critical point. What the dramatic effects will be as the Earth's atmosphere, land masses and oceans drift to a new dynamic is not exactly predictable. What we do know is that there has been a gradual warming and that this warming might accelerate if we do not curb both our behaviour and emissions of gaseous carbon products from the burning of fossil fuels. Thus many governments of nations across the world are struggling to alter their mind set and put in place alternative means of the production of electricity and energy generally. This is a particularly difficult task when such essential things in modern civilisation such as iron and steel production, glass and concrete all depend on emissions of oxides of carbon to be realised! Nuclear energy has provided an alternative but its waste is excessively polluting! Clean fusion has not been successful on a commercial scale to date. Battery production making use of lead, lithium and/or nickel also have problems of pollution if not cautiously recycled. Wind, solar, tidal, water potential and geothermal all have great advantages over the burning of gas, oil or coal provided electrical storage is not too great or too polluting. Thermal piles for heat energy storage are a worthwhile consideration. Just as there are holocaust deniers there are also climate change deniers. Only education and direct evidence can assist a portion of these. Some will remain forever unconvinced and like the lemming, luddite or dinosaur will follow the path to self destruction. There is little one can do to change the innate and possibly genetic makeup of the lemming!

AUSTRALIA

 Dinner & Info Night
Wed 10 May, 6pm
312 Smith St, Collingwood

Inspiration from Vegas, USA.

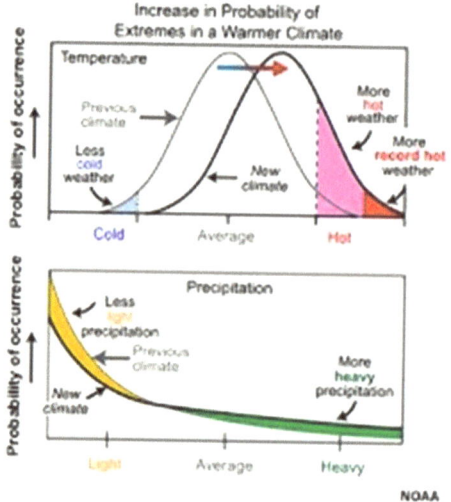

Previous climate compared with new climate

Retweet

Retweet   A.Gunner@alcgunn

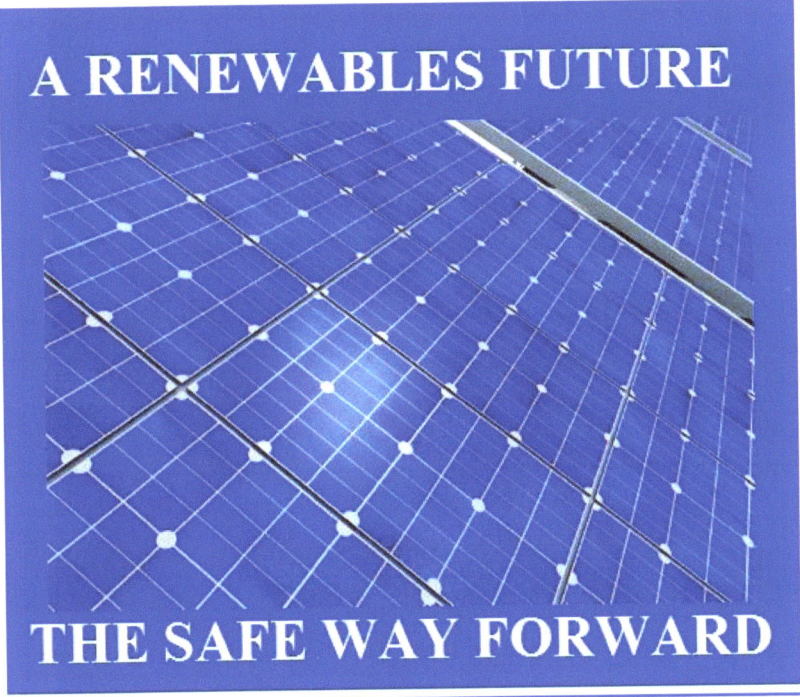

Greenland melt contributes to rise in sea levels on US East coast

More nations reaching critical point regarding carbon emissions !

New Zealand planning on 100% renewable by 2035 !

Retweets from PeterDGardner

Australia near bottom of list of nations attending to emissions !

Why is Australia slow in adopting use of Electric Cars ?

VII   *General*

There are so many other interesting and sometimes damaging things going on in the world that do not quite fit the first few classifications; and so I have shoved them here into a chapter called General! If I thought something was worth commenting on then I tweeted my praise or indignation. Examples might include President Duderte of the Philippines rampant street murders of suspected drug traders and dealers without the due process of law. The Myanmar exodus of the Rohingya people due to the military's policy of ethnic cleansing. Marine Le pen's attempt at power in France early in the year or the cruelty of Sharia Law in Ache Province of Indonesia. Events materialise that cannot be allowed to pass unnoticed or without some miniscule protest or comment! But the world and information gallop along at an overwhelming rate and it is impossible for the individual human brain to absorb, analyse and store away for future reference other than whatever seems to be personally relevant at the time. The reader may find some repetition of material here as elsewhere in the collection. One hopes that some thought provocation has occurred or merely some humorous nerve has been tweaked to cause a titter or outburst of laughter!

I will mention here that the final chapter includes a smattering of material that is not my own but which I found to be excessively offensive. I place these examples here not for the purpose of further offending my readers but to merely demonstrate the depth of depravity and hatefulness that some get away with on social media. There should be tighter controls, checks and balances on what is broadcast and published on social media so that such extreme materials can be quickly and decisively removed. As with graffiti of old painted on walls in the dead of night, society must be vigilant! "Romans Go Home!"

Turkey Dictator

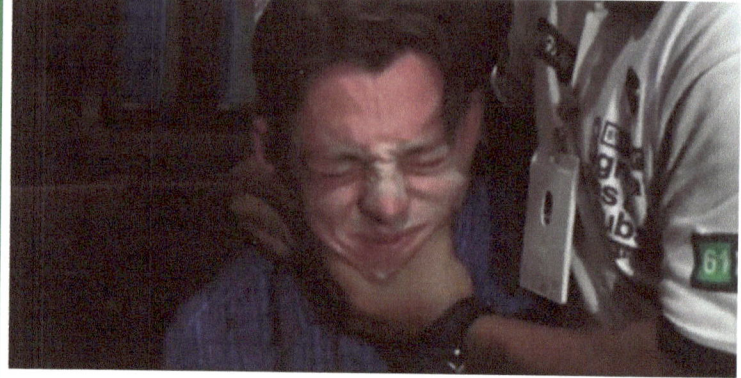

RUSSIAN ATTEMPTS TO THEORISE ON SYRIAN GAS ATTACKS POINTS TO THEIR COMPLICITY AFTER ALL, THE RUSSIAN MILITARY USED CHEMICAL ATTACKS IN AFGHANISTAN BETWEEN 1979 AND 1982 MORE THAN FORTY TIMES !!

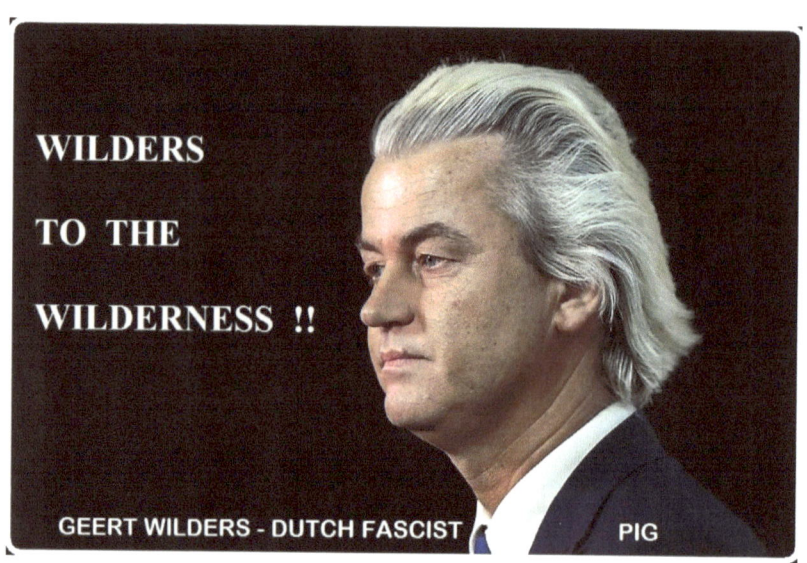

INDONESIA TO PLACE TRAVEL BAN ON TRUMP

AND FREEZE ALL HIS ASSETS ACROSS NATION

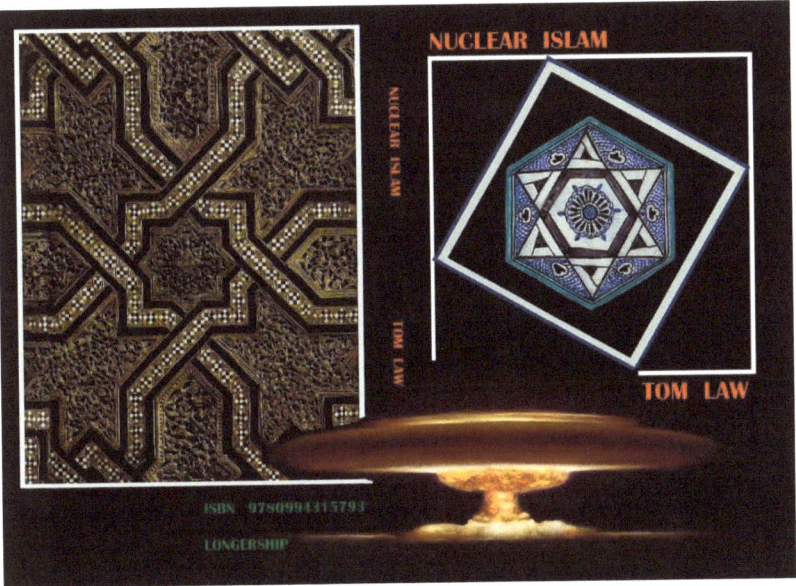

Ramadan ... pity IS and Sunni extremists have thrown away the true meaning of "peace and good will" to all ! SHAME

This duck will never become a swan !

LIVING TOGETHER

IN
PEACE & HARMONY

Sharia in Aceh Province, Indonesia

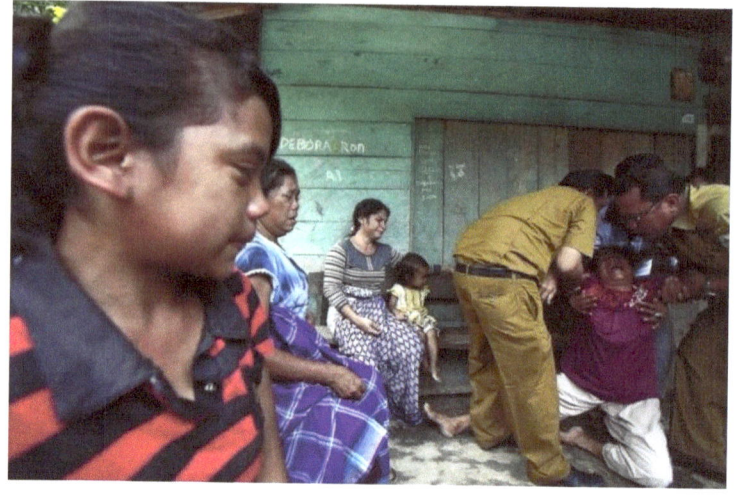

TURN RIGHT S'IL VOUS PLAIT: French peasants and prostitutes drive Ozzie girl from beach in La France Libre!

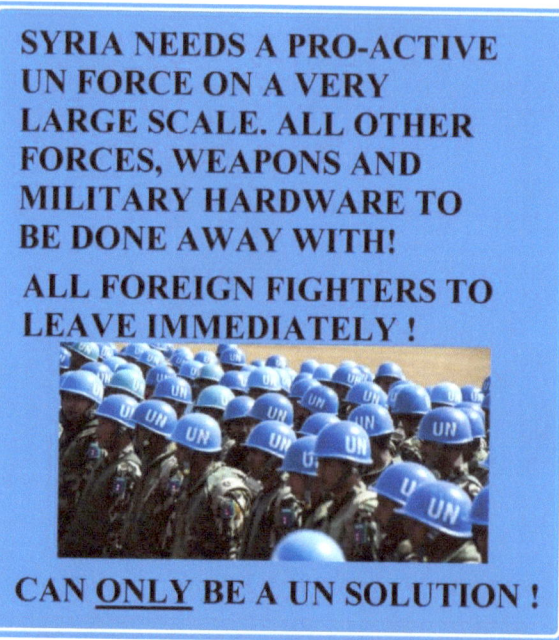

CHINA MOVES ON CHURCHES

FIRST YOU SEE IT...

THEN YOU DON'T !

Jakarta ex-Governor jailed for blasphemy!

Arschlechers !

Retweet

WHAT'S ALL THE FUSS OVER HEADSCARFS ?

Qu'est ce que l'agitation pour les foulards ?

THE BETSY RIOT PROCLAMATION OF 2017

WHEREAS love only trumps hate when love has fangs;

WHEREAS the high road is a nice vantage point for watching the world burn but trenches are where you fight;

THEREFORE BE IT RESOLVED that no neo-nazi fucker shall find peace or platform where any Betsy is present;

and no fascist pencil-pusher will enact the Trump agenda without a nasty fight; because

When they go low, we will kick them in the scrotum.

Retweet: Ha ha, Betsy.. you're the best and I love you !

VIII   *Cruel, Nasty and Definitely NOT Mine!*

As said earlier, Social Media has a lot to answer for and the owners of sites such as facebook, twitter etc. must be much more vigilant in taking down material deemed excessively offensive to the community at large. BUT what is excessive? Who shall be the judge? Are values and morality on the constant slide downwards? Whereas offensive material is in the realm of a country's laws and values our saving grace is that most material is seen by very small numbers of people. So the most vile anti-Semitic, anti-Muslim or other similar denigrating tweets rarely go virile, seen by only a few hundred persons. Never the less I have found that in many cases the vile tweet is launched frequently. This is disturbing! If laws are tightened so that even the owners of Servers as well as sites are able to be prosecuted, it might be a step in the right direction. But the www is a complicated and all pervasive beast. A transmission between terrorists might take a fraction of a second. Daily data runs into extraordinarily high figures across the world.. some 10^{14} bits each day.. how can so much be surveyed and by whom? But I still find it hard to fathom why ISIL and al Qaida are able to publish their putrid material online (Dabiq and Inspire respectively) and their materials not only be found via search engines such as google, but may be easily downloaded! It beggars belief!

So I have included a few bitter tweets in this chapter and again state forcefully that none of these are my own creations but those of sick minds. Millions appear each day and I submit just a sample for my readers to get the general gist of the evil and unwellness of the minds of some individuals that get some demented thrill at posting such material. Racism and bigotry exist as a failing and weakness of a section of humanity. Perhaps we all have some prejudices or values perceived as contemptuous by others and therefore need to exercise restraint!

Anti Semitic rubbish!

TV we can all do without if its anything like the original Romper Stomper !

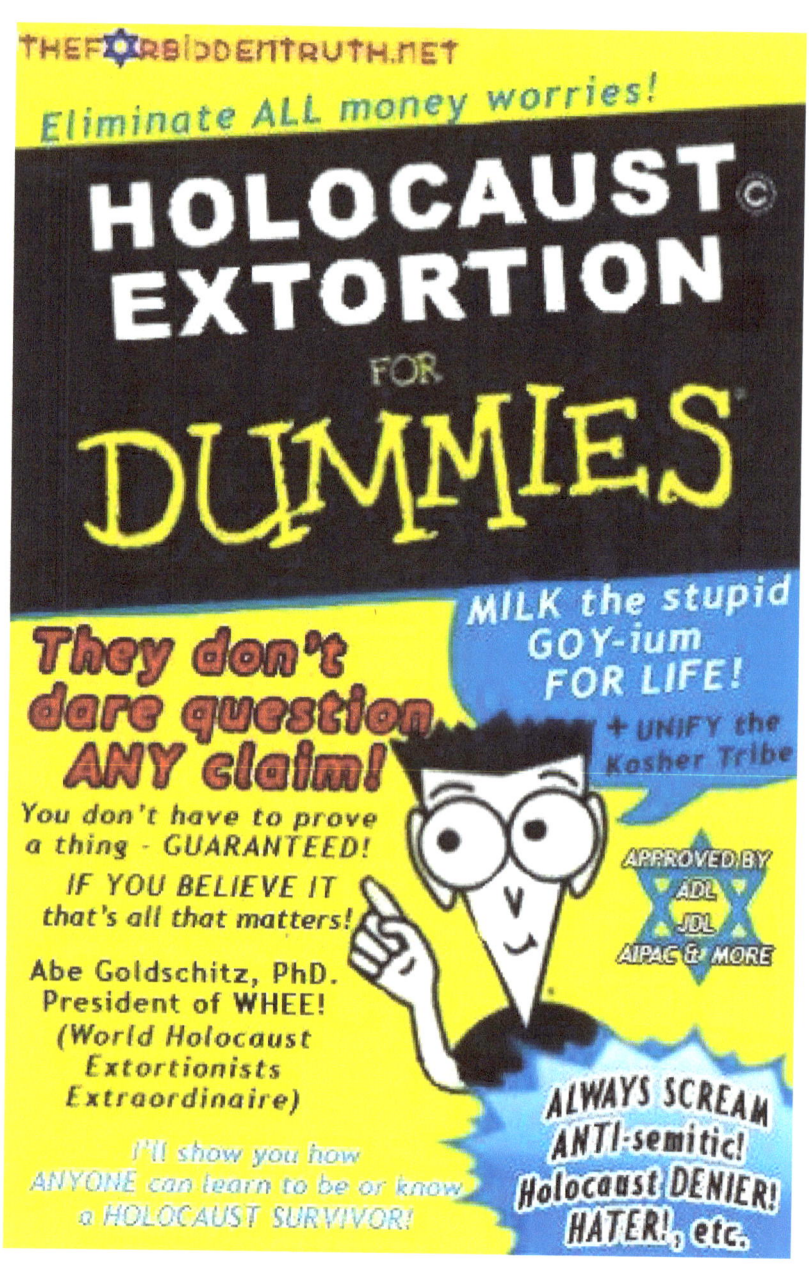

.. more of the same!

Fidelio@ Fidelio_is_weer

from smoloko.com

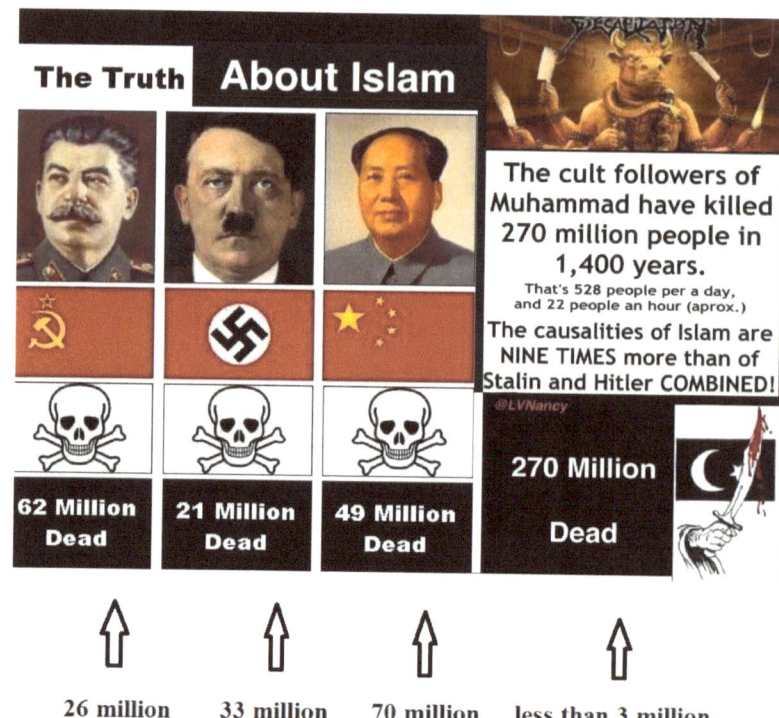

   26 million   33 million   70 million   less than 3 million

MORE REALISTIC NUMBERS !

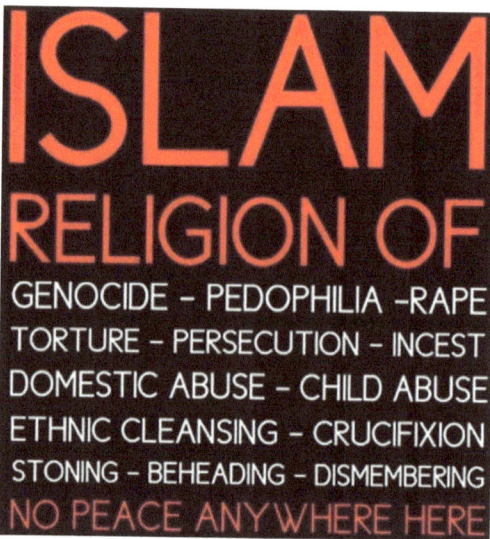

Same as Rome!

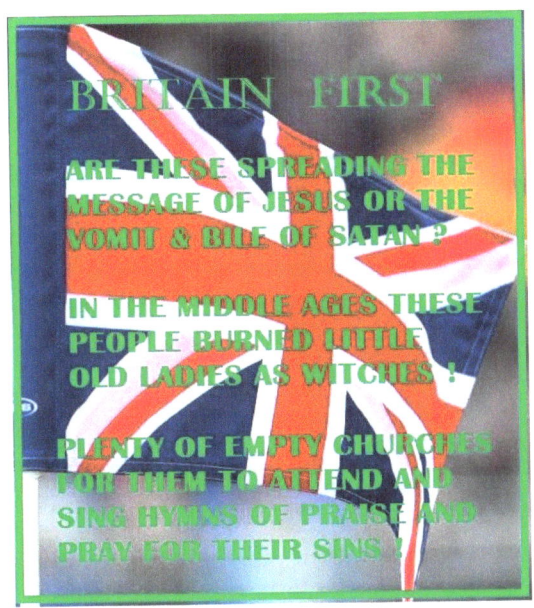

Unsigned !

Fuck white people and their fucking guns and their bullshit gun culture and all of it. Goddammit.

7/23/15, 10:44 PM

4 Retweets 9 Likes

Certainly over the top Megan !

Retweet: Maybe is unaware that 40 Americans are shot DEAD by their fellow Americans EVERY DAY .. it'd be too embarrassing to go into the figures on rape!

DEAR MUTTI -

SIMPLE SOLUTION:

"PLACE ALL THE AfD MEMBERS IN PRISON FOR THEIR DEPARTURE FROM THE CONSTITUTION !!"

THEN PROCEED TO GOVERN!

Refer

Sydney Morning Herald
The Age
Herald-Sun
New York Times
Daily Telegraph
ABC News 2 and 24
SBS News
images on line: various freebees
some twitter accounts:

    longershippubau
    RenewableepV
    PeterDGardner
    TomthunkitsMind
    AgendaOfEvil
    PersianRose1
    IndosiarID
    ParisMatch
    Swedish_girl80
    betsyriot
    I Spinner
    alcgunn
    blurtsy

Web:
auswp.org   Australian Workers Party
dec.org.uk   Disasters Emergency Committee
unclesamsmisguidedchildren.com
gunviolencearchive.org
longership.com
agendaofevil.com   anti Islamic rubbish
smoloko.com   Nazi site

Other Titles by Tom Law

Helter Skelter

ISBN   9780994315724

The title of 'Helter Skelter', Tom Law's latest book, almost speaks for itself. Basically, due to human folly, the writing leads us to the world's end with perhaps the survival of just a few reverting to a pre high tech existence. The storyline is interwoven with political outpourings, observations and graffiti ramblings. Sequence is a problem as factual narrative merges into drama, futuristic fantasy and prediction. So be warned: the flow is deceptive as the text is driven into cataracts, over waterfalls and through chasms lined with sharp rocks and oblique boulders. The writing is at times confused, abstract and didactic.. in other words, unconventional! Never the less, apart from being confronting it is a worthwhile read hopefully with lessons to be learned. Although the tome displays bucket loads of negativity and evil, the coda is a final escape route to the possibility of an alternative and possibly something better. Touches upon all the current problems and dilemmas facing humanity.

Available on all amazon sites and on Kindle:

https://www.amazon.com/Helter-Skelter-Tom-Law/dp/0994315724/

book UK:

https://www.amazon.co.uk/s/ref=nb_sb_noss/262-0909569-0867065

Kindle Australia :

https://www.amazon.com.au/s/ref=nb_sb_noss/355-4093848-9771003

Nuclear Islam   3rd Edition

ISBN   9780994315793

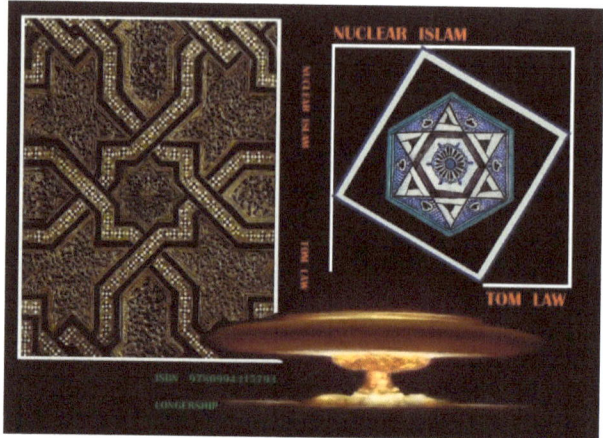

This expose on what our future holds if we continue down the nuclear road looks at the various scenarios from conventional nuclear power plants. Also discusses the causes and outcomes of Islamic terror and how we can heal the divisions between the various religions on the planet. Population expansion is beyond our control- taken together with finite resources, the planet faces some tough times ahead!

Return to Animalia

ISBN   9780994315700

Politics of contemporary Australia as seen through the eyes of perhaps a very British Australian. A disquieting diatribe on many issues with solutions given as possible suggestions. Could easily be construed as unapologetic extremism by some, but sensible remedies by others- depending on one's perspective!

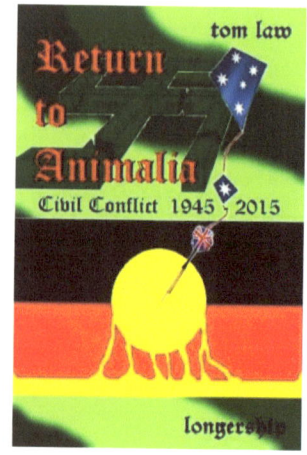

China Collection.

ISBN 9780980725889

This is a collection of four books of poetry by Tom Law on political and environmental observations written over a period of six years whilst working in Jiangsu province, China as a science teacher. It is a commentary on Chinese life, politics with a little romanticism thrown in. There are also references to world events over the period particularly the Middle East conflicts

Guns Off Cops Guns Off Everyone!

ISBN   9780994315779

A hard look at US policy on guns and the continual high rate of killings by guns in that country. Also describes the roll of the armaments industries in wars around the world and the development of the new weapons.

Tears from a Persian Rose

ISBN

An extremely short booklet containing the wisdom titled 'Tears from a Persian Rose'. It comprises a collection of religious phrases as a guide to the safety, well being and general happiness of humans living upon this Earth. Most of the advice (or perhaps better described as a series of life values) cannot be dated precisely and owe their origins to a variety of ancient works such as the Torah and Old Testament biblical scripts. The important thing to note is that, as far as human behaviour is concerned, they are timeless and have proven themselves to be a safe guide for the survival of human communities wherever they dwell now or have lived in the past. Modern times are no different from any epoch in human history and civilisation.

Get it on Kindle !

Available at: amazon.com   amazon.ca   amazon.co.uk   amazon.de   amazon.fr   amazon.it   amazon.es   amazon.in   amazon.co.jp   amazon.cn   amazon.id

.. also, for other titles by Tom Law please go to: longership.com

Retweet:

We just so want to be like you Americans and be in the movies too !!

www.ingramcontent.com/pod-product-compliance
Lightning Source LLC
Chambersburg PA
CBHW040302010526
44108CB00033B/4